do it NOW *do it* FAST *do it* RIGHT®

Containers

with Style

APR - 2006

do it NOW *do it* FAST *do it* RIGHT®

Containers
with Style

The Taunton Press

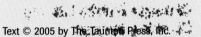

The Taunton Press
Inspiration for hands-on living®

The Taunton Press, Inc., 63 South Main Street, PO Box 5506, Newtown, CT 06470-5506

e-mail: tp@taunton.com

Distributed by Publishers Group West

WRITER AND PROJECT MANAGER: Jeff Day

EDITOR: Jennifer Renjilian Morris

SERIES EDITOR: Tim Snyder

SERIES DESIGN: Lori Wendin

LAYOUT: Potter Publishing Studios

ILLUSTRATOR: Charles Lockhart

COVER PHOTOGRAPH: Randy O'Rourke

LIBRARY OF CONGRESS CATALOGING-IN-PUBLICATION DATA

Containers with style.
    p. cm. -- (Do it now/do it fast/do it right)
  ISBN 1-56158-678-1
  1. Plant containers. 2. Container gardening. I. Series.
  SB418.4.C65 2004
  635.9'86--dc22
                              2004013151

Printed in the United States of America
10 9 8 7 6 5 4 3 2 1

Acknowledgments

WE'RE GRATEFUL TO THE manufacturers and experts whose talent and hard work made this book possible. Thanks to Joe Provey, Diana Baxter, John White, Roy Barnhart, Randy O'Rourke, Donna Chiarelli, Wendi Mijal, and Jennifer Peters. Thanks also to Peter's Garden of Quakertown, Pennsylvania, Stanley® Tools of New Britain, Connecticut, Freud Tools of High Point, North Carolina, and Robert Bosch™ Tools of Chicago, Illinois.

Contents

CONTAINER PROJECTS

Easy Embellished Pots 68

Turn ordinary clay pots into distinctive planters with **TILE, SHELLS, or PAINT**

How to Use This Book

I F YOU'RE INTERESTED IN HOME IMPROVEMENTS that add value and convenience while also enabling you to express your own sense of style, you've come to the right place. **Do it Now/ Do it Fast/Do it Right** books are created with an attitude that says "Let's get started!" and an ideal mix of home improvement inspiration and how-to information. Do it Now books don't skip important steps or force you to guess at what needs to be done to take a project from start to finish.

You'll find that this book has a friendly, easy-to-use format. (See the sample pages shown here.) You'll begin each project knowing exactly what tools and gear you'll need, and what materials to buy at your home center or building supply outlet. You can get started confidently because every step is illustrated and explained. Along the way, you'll discover plenty of expert advice packed into the margins. For ideas on how to personalize your project, check out the design options pages that follow the step-by-step instructions.

WORK TOGETHER

If you like company when you go to the movies or clean up the kitchen, you'll probably feel the same way about tackling home improvement projects. The

Get the TOOLS & GEAR you need. You'll also find out what features and details are important.

WHAT'S DIFFERENT? helps you decide which product to buy.

DO IT NOW helps to keep your project on track with timely advice.

COOL TOOL puts you in touch with tools that make the job easier.

WHAT TO BUY helps you put together your project shopping list so you get all the materials you need.

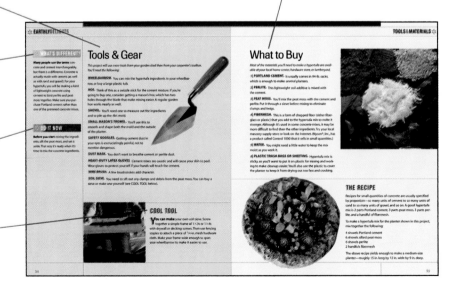

work will go faster, and you'll have a partner to share in the adventure. You'll see that some projects really call for another set of hands to help hold parts in place or keep the project going smoothly. Read through the project you'd like to tackle and note where you're most likely to need help.

PLANNING AND PRACTICE PAY OFF

Most of the projects in this book can easily be completed in a weekend. But the job can take longer if you don't pay attention to planning and project preparation requirements. Check out the conditions in the area where you'll be working. Chapter 1 (Get Set) will tell you about the tools and materials required for most of the projects in this book.

Your skill and confidence will improve with every project you complete. But if you're trying a technique for the first time, it's wise to rehearse before you "go live." This means ordering a little extra in the way of supplies and materials, and finding a location where you can practice your technique.

DESIGN OPTIONS
Personalize your project with dimensions, finishes, and details that fit your space and sense of style.

STEP BY STEP Get started, keep going, and finish the job. Every step is illustrated and explained.

WHAT CAN GO WRONG explains how to avoid common mistakes.

DO IT RIGHT tells you what it takes to get top-notch results.

Get Set

Here's what you need to know to create
great-looking **CONTAINER GARDENS**

WHETHER YOU'RE DRESSING UP the inside or the outside of your home, container gardens add a spark of color that almost nothing else can equal. Think of this chapter as an icebreaker—in it, you'll learn how to choose containers that match the needs of your plants while enhancing

your decor. You'll learn to select the tools and materials to create containers with panache. You'll also find what you need to know to grow great-looking container plants. The keys to success are all here.

Barrels, baskets, bowls, boxes, and anything else you can think of—including vintage hats and handbags—can become planters. If the containers don't have cracks or holes, drill drain holes. Wash them before using to remove dirt and to discourage plant diseases. Line wicker baskets, wooden boxes, and otherwise leaky containers with plastic trash bags before planting. Elevate wood and wicker on bricks to allow the bases to dry out between waterings and to prevent rot.

To protect plants from pests that hitch a ride on used pots, clean and disinfect containers before reusing. Soak dirty pots in a solution of 1 part household bleach to 10 parts water for 30 minutes. Then scrub them with a brush and rinse.

Size & Shape

TALL POTS, traditionally called "Long Toms," are best suited for deep-rooted plants, such as small trees and shrubs, and for long-rooted perennials like lilies and black-eyed Susans. Their elevated height also suits trailing plants, which can cascade gracefully over their edges. Hanging pots and baskets are specifically designed for cascading plants. Short pots, sometimes called bulb pans, are ideal for shallow-rooted flowering bulbs and ferns and for vines, which have spreading roots. Short pots also provide a broad surface area for grouping little gardens of plants with similar needs, such as a cacti and succulents. If you want to grow healthy begonias, bromeliads, and orchids, which are sometimes called "air plants" because they naturally grow in little or no soil, look for pots with ventilated sides, which allow adequate air circulation around their roots (see the photo below).

Choose a pot that is about one-third the height of the plant and about 4 in. larger in diameter than the pot your plant came in. In a year or two, when the roots grow to the point that they begin to circle the inside of the pot, it's time to "pot up" to a new pot that's 4 in. bigger than the one it's in, and so on.

WHETHER ELEGANT OR QUIRKY, all pots are designed to accommodate plants. The trick is in choosing among the thousands of planters available.

What to Buy

A STURDY FLOWERPOT can last a lifetime, or even several lifetimes, so feel free to shop for a pot at a flea market, use a family heirloom, or buy a new pot. Condition is ultimately what matters: Look for a pot with a flat bottom that won't easily tip over, and one without cracks. Make sure the pot has one or two drain holes so the soil can drain. Clay pots made in North America, Europe, and the Orient are less likely to crumble and crack in cold weather than those made in South America.

If you do happen to fall in love with a damaged pot, don't despair: You can still display plants in it. Put your plants in an inexpensive plastic pot and set it into the damaged pot. If the plastic pot is visible, hide it with a topping of decorative moss or pebbles. If you want to prolong the life of a cracked pot, run a bead of epoxy glue or silicone caulk over the crack on the inside of the pot where it won't show.

Like vases, decorative pots made of ceramic, clay, or wood are typically used to display plants indoors.

Concrete pots are weatherproof and won't tip over in strong winds, making them ideal for use on patios, parking areas, or in the garden.

Follow Tradition

DON'T THINK FOR A MINUTE that traditional equals boring when it comes to containers for your plants. You can find pots in almost any color and size, with or without decorative details. Some are handmade and come from Europe, and some are manufactured and come from down the road. You'll find something in every price range, too.

CLAY. Clay has been used for containers for centuries. Because it is mined from the earth, it provides a growing environment that closely replicates soil, making it a favorite of many gardeners. Clay walls are porous, allowing air to reach the roots and water to evaporate. This keeps roots cool in summer and makes the pots ideal for drought-tolerant plants, such as cacti. (To grow plants that need more water, you'll have to water frequently or add water-absorbing granules to the soil.) When properly cared for, clay pots have a sparse beauty that can last a lifetime, but they do break easily and are vulnerable to cracking if left outside year-round in cold climates.

CONCRETE & STONE. Concrete and stone pots are durable and frost proof, and their weight keeps them from tipping over in strong winds. Like clay,

You can choose from many sizes and styles of terra-cotta.

these pots are somewhat porous, so plants will need regular watering. They make a nice home for plants as big as shrubs and trees. Because of their weight, they are hard to move around and so are most often used outdoors as permanent landscape additions.

GLAZED CERAMIC. Glazed ceramic pots come in a dazzling array of styles and colors. Because of their beauty, cost, and fragility, they are most often used indoors.

METAL. Many metals are better for display than for actually growing plants. Some, such as copper and brass, can retard plant growth if allowed to come into contact with the soil, and most will rust or corrode in time. Even galvanized metal will rust, though it takes longer than untreated metal. Metal containers get very hot in the sun and overheat plants, so these containers should be kept in the shade.

WOOD. Wooden planters come in shapes from the classic Versailles box to casual window boxes and even fruit crates. Cedar and redwood are used most for planters because they naturally resist rot and insects. Pressure-treated wood works equally well in planters, but you must take extra safety precautions when working with it, and you might not want to plant edibles in it. Lining the planters with plastic before planting also helps prevent rot. (You can buy plastic liners to fit most planter sizes.) You can also prime and paint wood for added protection.

A tall ceramic pot makes an elegant statement and elevates a short plant to eye level.

To extend the life of a wooden planter, use a rot-proof plastic liner.

Potted plants can overheat if they are placed in hot summer sun, especially if they are in a dark-colored pot. Insulate the roots by buying a pot with a diameter that is 2 in. to 3 in. bigger than the plants require and line it with one or two layers of bubble wrap. Try rigid foam insulation sheets for square or rectangular pots. Be careful not to block the drain hole. Plant the pot as usual.

Make It Modern

LIGHTWEIGHT & INEXPENSIVE, pots made from modern synthetic materials look like their traditional counterparts but have some advantages. You can move them easily, they weather well, and you can get almost any look you want. You have to watch how much you water because the pots are not porous, but these pots are unsurpassed for growing moisture-loving plants like ferns.

COMPOSITES & POLYRESIN. Composite and polyresin pots are lightweight synthetic newcomers that replicate the look and texture of hand-carved stone, weathered and mossy concrete, or even the patina of old plaster, copper, or bronze. These pots are frost resistant and durable, and they provide some insulation at only a fraction of the cost of the real thing.

FIBERGLASS. Fiberglass is also used to duplicate classic pots. These non-porous pots are frost-resistant and lightweight, but the walls are thin and provide little insulation.

Durable polyresin and polystyrene foam pots replicate their classical but more fragile terra-cotta cousins at a fraction of the cost.

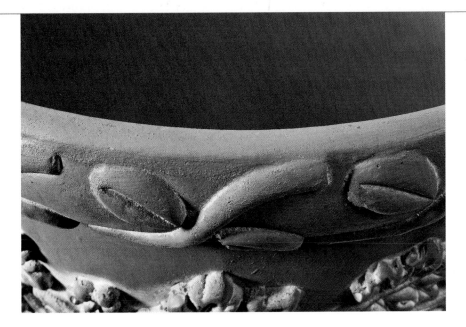

The thick foam walls of polystyrene pots insulate plant roots against hot sun and freezing winter temperatures.

FOAM OR POLYSTYRENE. Foam or polystyrene pots are lightweight, inexpensive, and nonporous. They come in many shapes and finishes. Their thick walls protect plants during cold winters and hot summers. Because they are lightweight, they may need to be weighed down or staked in windy sites.

PLASTIC. Plastic pots are lightweight, inexpensive, and hold moisture well. There are plastic pots to match almost any style, from beadboard to clay. Look for pots labeled as UV treated. They stand up to strong sunlight and won't overheat the soil and roots. These lightweight pots might also need weights or stakes in windy sites.

RUBBER. Rubber has recently been recycled into flexible, nonporous pots that withstand freezing and are heavy enough to withstand moderate winds without toppling.

Flexible rubber pots are nearly unbreakable, and weighty enough to resist toppling in wind.

⁑ DO IT FAST

A cordless, handheld vacuum makes short work of cleaning up spilled soil, plant snippings, and other small debris, whether it's still on your worktable or has escaped to the floor. If you already have one, plug it into an outlet near the potting bench.

⏵ DO IT RIGHT

Don't pot plants in the kitchen or utility sink—unless you want to invite the plumber over. Sand and soil can quickly clog a drain. Instead, do the potting on a table protected with newspapers or a tarp—and take newly potted plants outdoors for watering.

Covering the potting table with several layers of newspaper makes cleanup a snap; just roll up and dispose of the top layer of papers between projects.

Where to Work

GETTING A WORK STATION TOGETHER can mean the difference between being a clean potting machine or the mud-flinging horticultural equivalent of a monster-truck rally. A worktable, a place to store your potting gear, and a water source are essential. You don't have to have lots of bells and whistles or a lot of room. Something as simple as a picnic table outdoors or a card table in the garage or basement will do, too.

SETTING IT UP. To outfit an outdoor potting area, consider investing in one of the many handsome manufactured potting benches, or appropriate the picnic table and store your tools in a trunk or bucket with a snug-fitting lid. Indoors, install a pegboard and hooks on the wall for tools and shelves near your indoor worktable for watering cans, fertilizers, and floral supplies. Wherever your potting bench is, don't forget to keep a supply of water handy for cleanups and for watering newly potted plants. This can be as simple as a one-quart watering can for small jobs, a bucket of water and a ladle for medium jobs, or a garden hose for big jobs.

CONTROLLING THE MESS. An ounce of prevention is really the best way to control the mess, and it can be as simple as covering your worktable with several layers of newspapers. Newspapers are a wonderful covering, not only because they're free and biodegradable, but also because they provide a sterile surface

A watering can with a long, narrow spout makes it easy to direct water in tight places.

that won't transmit plant diseases. As you complete one planter, simply roll up and dispose of the top layer of paper before starting the next. Toss used papers into the compost bin, where they'll turn into next year's mulch.

When messes happen, relax. Into every potting room a little dirt must fall. Reach for a cordless vacuum or a dustpan and brush. If you are working in a garage or shed, you can make short work of cleaning up with a shop vacuum or with a well-aimed leaf blower. Keep a soft-bristled paintbrush handy for dusting intricately textured pots and fuzzy-leafed plants. Use a spray bottle of water and a soft cloth to wipe smooth-leaved plants and slick-sided pots.

In warm weather, move your potting operation to the picnic table and let the dirt fall where it may.

A meter for measuring soil pH gives an instant reading of soil acidity or alkalinity and comes with a chart listing plants and their pH needs. With it you can check your soil and make adjustments so your plants will flourish.

Inhaling soil and compost particles can aggravate allergies and pose a health problem for those with asthma. Do your potting in a well-ventilated place, preferably outdoors. Wear an inexpensive paper dust mask, and toss and replace it with each potting session. Those with two straps provide a better seal against dust.

The Gardener's Tool Kit

TO MAKE CONTAINER PLANTING FUN & EFFICIENT, you'll need a basic collection of garden tools and materials. To avoid dashing to the garden center in the middle of a project, stock up on the items listed here.

TOOLS

A few good-quality, basic tools can serve several functions and will last a lifetime. When shopping for sturdy-handled tools, look for those that are cast in one piece or that have a forged steel shank extending from the blade into the handle. Inexpensive, stamped-metal blades that wrap around the handle can bend, rust, and break.

ROOT SAW OR SERRATED KNIFE. Keep a thick-bladed tool with a serrated edge handy for cutting through the tangled roots of hanging baskets and perennials that need to be cut down to size.

TROWEL. To avoid frustration and making a muddy mess, buy a narrow-bladed trowel for digging planting holes.

SCOOPS. Scoops are cheap, so buy lots of them in different sizes and keep one in each bag of soil, perlite, and other potting amendments. Use a small scoop to fill in the gaps around plant stems and roots of potted plants to keep the foliage clean.

LATEX GLOVES. You can buy disposable latex gloves in boxes of 100 for about $10. When handling sand, gravel, or thorny plants, you'll be glad to have extras on hand.

PRUNING SHEARS. Get bypass pruners, which have a scissors action, because they make clean cuts that look good and heal quickly.

UTILITY SCISSORS. Keep a pair of utility or kitchen scissors handy for trimming delicate stems and cutting off dead flowers.

WATERING CAN. A long, straight spout makes watering easier in tight spots, in places where you have to reach over something, or when watering hanging baskets.

MATERIALS

In addition to the basic tools, there are some materials that you should have on hand.

SLOW-RELEASE FERTILIZER PELLETS. A handful of these pellets will ensure that plants receive nutrients with each watering during an entire season.

MOISTURE-RETAINING CRYSTALS. Using these crystals means you have to water less and keeps potted plants healthier in hot weather. Wet them before mixing them into the soil.

NEWSPAPER. Cover your worktable with several layers of newspaper. Roll up and throw out the top layer after you've finished one pot so you'll have a sterile surface for the next pot.

PERLITE. Perlite is used to lighten soil and provide superior drainage. Add more or less depending on whether the plants need a moist or a well-drained soil.

SOIL OR SOILLESS MIX. You can mix your own soil-based potting medium from potting soil or bagged topsoil, or buy a commercial soilless mix, which is peat-moss based. Soil-based mixes tend to hold moisture better than soilless mixes and are a natural source of nutrients. Soilless mixes usually weigh less.

Keep a scoop in every bag of soil amendment, and use rubber-coated or latex gloves to save wear and tear on your hands when potting.

Bypass pruners have a scissors action that produces clean-edged cuts, which allow plants to heal fast.

❋ WHAT'S DIFFERENT?

Deck screws have a coarse, sharp
thread and are similar to drywall
screws. Use them on any project that
goes outdoors. Unlike drywall
screws, they're either galvanized or
ceramic coated to keep them from
rusting. Both coatings work well, but
ceramic coatings are more durable. If
you use galvanized screws, get hot-
dipped galvanized screws rather
than electroplated, because the
coating is thicker.

The Builder's Tool Kit

YOU'LL NEED HAND TOOLS & POWER TOOLS to build the projects in this
book. Here's what to look for:

TAPE MEASURE. Get one with a ¾-in.-wide blade; it won't bend when
you're trying to measure long distances. A 16-footer is long enough,
but longer tapes come in handy if you ever have to measure rooms in
the house.

HAMMER. Get a 16-oz. curved-claw hammer. A wooden handle is
traditional, cheaper, and some say it transfers less shock to your
hand and elbow.

SQUARES. A **combination square** works for laying out corners and for
testing whether the sides really are perpendicular. Use a **speed square** to
guide a circular saw and cut a straight line. For those few times you want
to cut a piece at an angle, lay out the line with a **sliding T-bevel**.

DRILL. A power drill is the first power tool you should buy. You'll find
yourself driving screws with it nearly as often as you drill holes, so buy a
magnetic screwdriver bit in addition to a set of **twist drills**. Most drill
chucks only open to a maximum of ⅜ in., so use **butterfly bits** with their
narrow shanks to drill larger holes.

You'll need a **countersink/counterbore** bit to drill pilot holes
and a cone-shaped recess for the screw head.

CIRCULAR SAW. A lumberyard or home center will cut
wood to size for you—for a price. But cutting boards
at home yourself is easy with a circular saw. Use it
carefully with guides in order to get straight cuts.

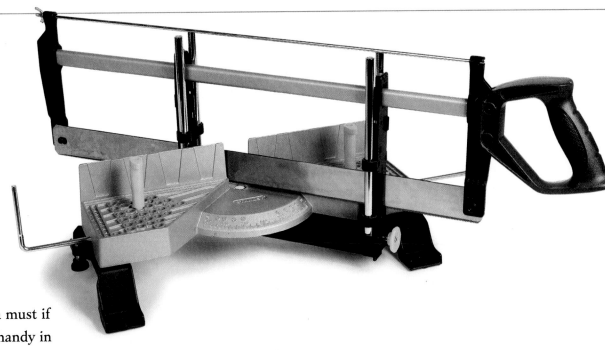

If a project has molding on it, you'll need to miter the ends—cut them at an angle—so that the molding flows from one side to the next without interruption. For small jobs, a hand miter box, shown here, does the trick.

MITER SAW. A miter saw is a must if you're cutting molding and handy in a lot of other situations. A power miter saw, also called a chopsaw, can be pricey but is worth it if you do a lot of work with moldings. If you don't want to spend the money, rent one for the day. Or if you're going to only do a little bit of molding work, consider a miter box with a handsaw. Get something like the one shown in the photo above. Wooden and plastic boxes lose accuracy with use.

JIGSAW. Indispensable when cutting curves, a jigsaw will also cut moderately straight lines.

The jigsaw's forte is cutting curves. You can also cut straight lines with it, but don't expect the lines to be perfect.

A horticultural light meter is a handheld sensor available at garden centers and from mail-order catalogs. This tool will take the guesswork out of measuring light. It comes with a booklet listing hundreds of plants and their light needs, making it easy to match plants with the light intensity in any area.

Before you buy a plant, check the foliage. Healthy foliage should not be wilted, and it should show signs of new growth. Look for fresh, bright green buds or new stems. Look for unopened flower buds on blooming plants. Mature foliage should be bright or deep green, unless it is a special yellow-leaved plant variety. Turn leaves over and check the undersides: Pass up any plants that have leaves infested with small insects or signs of chewing or fine spiderwebs.

Choose the Right Plants

MOST GARDEN CENTERS group their plants according to sunlight requirements, so once you know which kind of plant you need, shopping is a snap. Study the patterns of sunlight and shade as the sun moves across your patio, deck, or balcony to decide whether you need plants suited to full sun or shade-tolerant ones, and you're good to go.

IDEAS & INSPIRATION. Bulbs, annuals, perennials, and even small trees and shrubs can be grown in containers, and you can mix and match them to create stunning combinations. If you'd like an all-season display, create a vertically layered planter. Start with spring bulbs. Look for large bulbs, such as tulips and hyacinths, which should be planted deeply, and set them at the proper depth and cover with the recommended layer of soil. Then top them with later-emerging perennials, such as hostas and bleeding heart, daylilies,

Perennials, herbs, and even shrubs can be potted and grouped together to form a colorful patio garden.

peonies, or hydrangeas, and rim the edge of the pot with trailing evergreens, such as English Ivy or spreading junipers. Fill in around them with soil, leaving space for tucking in some colorful, season-long blooming annuals like impatiens, coleus, or portulaca. The bulbs will bloom in early spring, and the later emerging perennial leaves will hide their withering foliage. Bleeding heart and peonies bloom in early summer, and daylilies and hydrangeas will brighten the dog days of summer.

MATCHING POT & PLANT. Most plants can grow in containers, as long as the pots are big enough to accommodate the plants' roots. If you plan to display the plants for only one season, you can use a container that's not much bigger in diameter than the total diameter of all the companion plants grouped together. If you want to grow a small tree or shrub, plan to knock it out of the pot every other year and trim off a third of the roots and then repot it to keep it from becoming fatally rootbound.

Succulents and cacti grow slowly and can live happily for several years in small containers.

Despite their reputation as prima donnas, orchids are easily grown in containers.

Mix it up with style and a sense of humor, combining colorful flowering plants in a variety of reclaimed containers.

19

To knock plants from their nursery pots, hold your hand over the soil, turn the pot upside down, and, using your free hand, rap the rim of the pot against the edge of the table.

Perennials make great container plants. Before the onset of winter, be sure to remove the plants from their pots and plant them in the ground. Then simply repot them in the spring.

Keys to Success

PLANTS NEED JUST A FEW THINGS to thrive in pots—the right soil mix, adequate drainage, some fertilizer, enough water, and minor pest control.

DIRT. You want a soil mix that has enough compost or peat moss to hold moisture and enough coarse particles, such as perlite or sand, to allow drainage and circulation. You can buy ready-made potting soil, which meets the average needs of the average plant. But you can also make your own soil mix, customizing to the types of plants you're growing. An all-purpose mixture is one-third soil, one-third compost or peat moss, and one-third perlite or sand. If you are growing moisture-loving plants, such as ferns, add more compost or peat moss; if you're growing succulents and cacti, add perlite or sand.

DRAINAGE. Your pot needs at least one drain hole so that water can drain and your roots won't rot. If your pot doesn't have one, you'll need to make one. Use a spade bit that will create a hole at least ½ in. in diameter. Turn the pot upside down and drill the hole in the center of the pot. For large pots, use a larger bit or drill additional holes. Remember to poke holes in any plastic liner you add as well.

If your container does not have a drain hole, drill one with a spade bit that is at least ¹/₂ in. in diameter. Drill slowly to keep from cracking the pot.

Slow-release fertilizer comes in spikes, pellets, or organic solutions such as fish emulsion and liquid kelp.

Most insect pests can be killed by dabbing them with a cotton ball soaked in rubbing alcohol.

FOOD. Plant nutrition is critical to potted plants because they cannot send roots into the soil in search of nutrients. To ensure healthy plants, apply slow-release fertilizers at potting time. Keep a watchful eye on your plants; if the leaves turn pale and flowering slows, you may need to give them a boost of a fertilizer that dissolves in water. You don't want to overfertilize, though, so wait until you see a problem before you add more fertilizer. If you see a white, crusty deposit building up on the pot rim or surface of the soil, stop fertilizing and flush the pot with plain water.

WATER. When watering, pour tepid water over the soil until it drains from the pot. To find out if it's time to water, insert a finger into the soil up to the second knuckle. If the soil feels damp, wait a day or two and test again. If the soil feels dry, it's time to water.

PEST PATROL. Pest patrol is easy with potted plants because with each watering you get to look at them up close and personal. At the first sign of creepy-crawlies, hose the tops and undersides of the leaves with a strong stream of water. Rinsing the plants twice weekly for two or three weeks will clean off most pests and their eggs. But if that fails, you may spray ornamental plants (and some food plants) with commercial insecticidal soap. Follow the directions on the package.

A Garden in a Box

This basic window box brings THE OUTDOORS IN

PERFECT WHETHER YOU LIVE IN THE CITY OR COUNTRY, a window box creates a place for a garden even if you have no ground space. You can plant colorful flowers practically year-round and even add color during winter with holly, berries, and evergreens. This window box is easy to build and is lined with a plastic planter box, so you don't have to worry about rot. You don't need to search for inspiration. Just search for places that would benefit from flowers and a box to hold them. Before you know it you'll be admiring your boxed garden from inside and out.

CUT IT OUT   MAKE A CURVE   ASSEMBLE   HANG IT UP

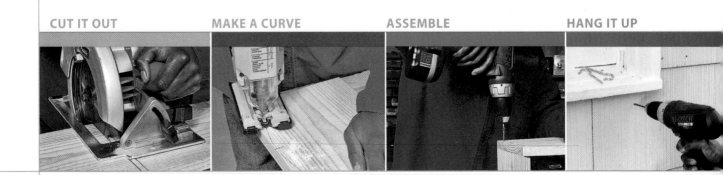

Match your window box to your window. The window box should be about as long as your window, measured from side to side, including the wood trim. If you can't get a plastic liner the same size as the window box, get one a little smaller, but build the planter to match the window's measurements. Wedge the liner in place with some wood scraps or stones.

WHAT CAN GO WRONG

You want straight boards, or your box won't fit together properly. To find straight boards, look down the edges of each one you intend to buy. Look for straight (as in arrow) rather than bow (as in leg) when you make your selections.

Tools & Gear

You don't actually need *all of this gear, but the more of it you have, the better the results are likely to be. You'll, of course, need the basics, like your hammer, a pencil, and tape measure.*

COMBINATION SQUARE. You'll put this to use laying out square cuts and measuring.

CIRCULAR SAW. A circular saw will give you a straighter, truer cut than a jigsaw.

JIGSAW. You'll need a jigsaw to cut out the curved ends of the window box. You can make all the other cuts with the jigsaw, too, but cutting a straight line is easier with a circular saw. Use a fine-toothed, wood-cutting blade in order to get the smoothest cuts.

CLAMPS. You've got only two hands. Get at least as many clamps. Ripping boards to width is a lot easier and safer when you clamp the board in place.

DRILL/DRIVER & BITS. You'll need a drill to make the pilot holes for the screws. You can also use it as a screwdriver. Get a combination countersink/counterbore bit to make drilling easy.

COOL TOOL

If you're cutting along the length of a board (called ripping), you want a rip guide for your circular saw. The guide is a small attachment that slips into a shoe somewhere on the saw. Lock the guide in place, and then feed it along the edge of the board to make a straight, even cut.

What to Buy

1| LUMBER. All you'll need is a single 1-in. × 8-in. × 8-ft. piece of pine. Look for a straight, flat board with as few knots as possible. You may want to splurge and get a piece of premium-grade lumber. The better grades of lumber tend to have fewer knots and be somewhat straighter.

2| DECK SCREWS. You'll need about twenty 2½-in. deck screws to assemble the window box.

3| SANDPAPER. You'll need 120-grit paper to prep the box for painting.

4| EXTERIOR PRIMER & PAINT. Prime and paint to create the look you want.

5| HOOKS & EYES. The way you hang your window box depends on what kind of siding is on your house. For vinyl, aluminum, and wooden clapboard siding, hang the box with a pair of hooks driven through the siding into the studs. Screw a set of corresponding eyes to the window box. Get hooks that are at least ¼ in. in diameter, 2½ in. long, and weather resistant. The eyes should be similar, but they only have to be 1½ in. long.

6| BRACKETS. If your house has brick, plywood, or other flat siding, you may be able to mount your window box on a pair of L-brackets. In this case, you'll need to purchase the brackets plus the necessary screws and anchors to mount them to your house. Buy a hook threaded for metal and then get an anchor to fit it.

7| CAULK. Whenever you put a hole in the siding of your house, caulk it. Get an exterior latex/silicone caulk, and spend the extra few cents to get whichever one is guaranteed the longest.

8| PLANTER BOX LINER. Lining your wood window box with a plastic planter box will keep it from rotting. Plastic planter boxes come in a variety of lengths. The one used here is 5 in. deep, 8 in. wide, and 30 in. long.

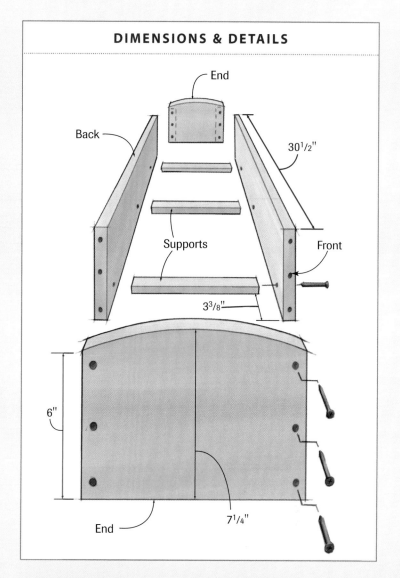

DIMENSIONS & DETAILS

Building the Box

1 **LAY IT OUT.** Use a combination square to help you mark layout lines for all four pieces. Measure the width of the front and back pieces (they're both 6 in.). The side pieces are already the right width. To measure, hold a pencil at the end of the ruler on your combination square and slide the square along the edge of the board. Mark the ends of each of the planter pieces on the line you've just drawn, allowing at least 1/4 in. between pieces for the width of the saw blade. Draw lines through the marks with a pencil and square. You will cut along these lines with the saw.

2 **CUT TO LENGTH.** Use your circular saw to cut the pieces to length. Position the blade so it just nicks the layout line as you cut and use a speed square as a guide.

3 **CUT TO WIDTH.** Clamp one of the pieces to the bench with a board underneath and the layout line overhanging the board. Put the rip-fence attachment on your circular saw. Set it so that when you guide the fence along the edge of the board the blade will be on the waste side of the cutting line. Move the clamps as necessary during the cut. Repeat on the remaining pieces. Save your scraps for the supports (see step 6).

4 **CUT THE END CURVES.** Lay out a curve by flexing a thin piece of wood, a flexible ruler, or even stiff poster board into a profile you like. Trace along it to mark your cutting line. It's important not to distort the curve while tracing along it. (You can use nails to hold the strip in place as you trace.) Remove the wood strip, then cut along the curve with a jigsaw.

▶ DO IT RIGHT

For strength, the hooks holding your window box should go into the studs. Find the studs from inside the house with an electronic stud finder. Measure where the studs are in relation to the center of the window, then measure again from outside, and mark the stud location on the siding.

❋ DO IT NOW

In brick walls, you'll need to drill a hole and install a fastener called an anchor to hold the hook in place. Drill the holes with a masonry bit. The size of the holes will depend on the size of the anchor you use. When you buy the anchors, ask what size hole they require, and buy a matching bit.

Hanging the Box

5 **GET IT TOGETHER.** Start by joining one end piece to the front piece. To keep the pieces steady while you attach them, clamp them together. Mark three screw holes on the end piece. Drill pilot holes with a combination countersink/counterbore bit, then screw the pieces together. Repeat on the remaining end and back pieces, then screw the two halves of the box together.

6 **INSTALL SUPPORTS.** Cut three supports from the scraps left over from cutting the front and back to width. Cut them so they fit snugly between the front and back pieces. Put one support near each end of the planter and one in the center (see the illustration on p. 25). Drill pilot holes for the screws. Screw the supports in place so they're flush with the bottom edge of the box. The box is now done. Sand with 120-grit sandpaper to smooth out the curved ends and prepare the box for painting.

7 **HANG THE HOOKS.** If your house has vinyl, aluminum, or wood clapboard siding, drill pilot holes for the hanger hooks through the siding into the studs (see DO IT RIGHT at left). Screw the hooks into the holes, then apply caulk carefully around the hooks where they enter the siding to prevent leakage. On brick siding, drill a hole large enough for a metal anchor, put the anchor in place, and then thread the hook into the anchor.

8 **INSTALL THE EYES.** Hold the box in place under the hooks and mark the hook locations on the edge of the box. Drill pilot holes $\frac{1}{16}$ in. smaller than the diameter of the hook, and screw the eyes in place (using a metal rod helps you keep a grip on the eye). Hang the window box on the hooks. The box will probably tilt forward a bit since it's attached only at the top. If you don't like this look, you can screw a piece of wood to the back at the bottom of the box so that the box doesn't slope forward. You're all set now to prime and paint. Then put the liner in and start planting.

5

6

7

8

A long, narrow window box planter works well on a porch or deck railing. This one simply sits atop the corner of two sides of the deck.

Make a planter with sloping sides by cutting the ends of the box at an angle. For a rustic-looking box, use rough-sawn cedar, shown here. For a contemporary look, buy cedar with planed surfaces.

The typical mailbox post is pretty basic. What better way to dress it up than with a window box–style planter? Add a rail to the back of the post, and then attach the planter to the rail.

A window box is simple enough to use anywhere, in any way, shape, or form. You can modify it to match the trim on your house, your color scheme, or your own sense of style. Add a little molding to give the box a Victorian touch or paint it bright turquoise for a Caribbean flavor.

Window boxes don't have to look pretty just in the summer. Add evergreens and holly for the winter season to make the box look festive from indoors and out.

A planter doesn't have to be rectangular. Commercially made hayrack planters have curved iron arms that you line with cocoa mats and plant just like the hanging planters on pp. 60–67.

▶ **DO IT RIGHT**

Take care to apply enough construction adhesive, but not too much. For these joints, parallel ¼-in. beads are just the right amount. Should some glue squeeze out, don't wipe it up or you may have a mess on your hands. Allow the glue to dry and peel it away with a sharp knife.

LINGO

A cleat is a narrow board that's used to join two sides that would otherwise be difficult to join directly, such as the tiles shown here.

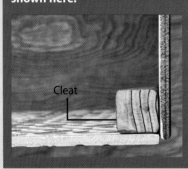

Cleat

Tools & Gear

MITER SAW. A miter saw allows you to make cross cuts and miter cuts.

CAULKING GUN. This convenient tool is used for applying adhesive.

CLAMPS. An assortment of spring clamps and Quick-Grip® clamps will make this project go faster. C-clamps will get the job done as well but will take more time.

SQUARES. You'll need both a combination and a framing square. They are essential tools in any workshop, so if you don't own them, now is a good time to buy them.

DRILL. You'll need a drill to assemble the pieces. It's best to have a drill with a clutch to help prevent sinking screws too deep when joining the trim frames to nailers.

FOAM BRUSH. Foam brushes are inexpensive and fine for a project like this. Polyester or nylon brushes will generally deliver better results.

COOL TOOL

A **miter clamp** is a clever invention that allows you to apply pressure to a miter joint. Simply place the pieces to be joined in the clamp and apply pressure as you would with a C-clamp screw. Miter clamps also act as a third hand should you need to hold two perpendicular workpieces together during assembly. A set of four clamps will speed the job, although you can get by with just one clamp if you're not in a big hurry.

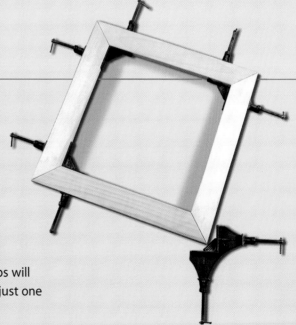

What to Buy

1| BALUSTER. Pressure-treated baluster (used for deck railings) is a good material for the cleats and nailers. It resists rot despite the direct contact with moist soil. But if you prefer not to handle pressure-treated wood, use 2×2 fir and prevent rot by lining the inside walls of the planter with heavy-mil black plastic.

2| CONSTRUCTION ADHESIVE. Look for a polyurethane adhesive that is odorless, easy to clean with soap and water, and that forms a strong bond. You can buy it in a large tube to use in a caulking gun, or you can buy it in a smaller container that can be hand-squeezed. With the smaller container, you'll have less leftover adhesive as well.

3| GLOVES. Protect your skin from the adhesive with rubber or vinyl gloves.

4| TILE. Really nice tile is expensive, especially if you must buy it by the carton. Save money by asking for tiles on clearance, samples of discontinued lines, or material left over from a tiling job. The tiles don't all have to be the same color, but they do need to be the same size. This project uses 18-in. × 18-in. tiles.

5| PAINTER'S TAPE. This type of tape will peel off without leaving a residue on your tile.

6| 1-FT. × 3-FT. × 8-FT. BOARDS. You'll need two 1-ft. × 3-ft. × 8-ft. boards to make the trim frames. You can use pine, cedar, or fir.

7| BRADS. Unless you have miter clamps, you'll need 1½-in. brads to hold the miter joints together as they dry.

8| CORNER MOLDING. The corner molding protects the tile edges from getting banged and chipped. It's optional if you prefer to see more of the tile.

9| PRESERVATIVE. Untreated parts, such as the trim frames, will last longer if you apply a couple of coats of preservative to them before screwing them to the nailers.

10| WATER-BASED STAIN. Water-based stains come in many shades and colors. They are easy to clean up but each coat must be applied rapidly and carefully in a single session to avoid a blotchy final appearance.

11| SCREWS. Look for 1⅝-in. galvanized or stainless steel exterior screws. The latter will be more expensive but will outlast the project.

12| CASTERS. Ball-type casters will handle the weight of most planters. Wheel-type casters are more industrial looking.

13| BOTTOM SLATS. For the bottom slats, you can use any type of scrap wood or buy a 10-ft. board if you don't have any scrap.

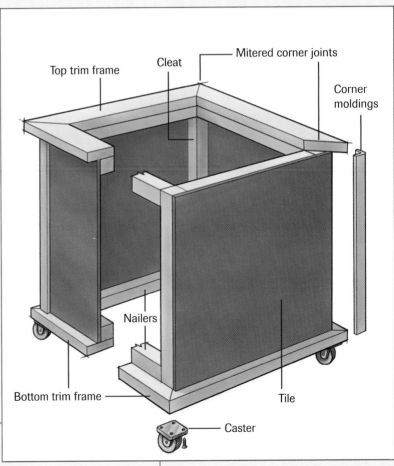

Top trim frame • Cleat • Mitered corner joints • Corner moldings • Nailers • Bottom trim frame • Tile • Caster

You can use C-clamps to hold the cleats and nailers to the tiles while the adhesive sets, but protect the tile edges from being chipped or cracked with wood pads cut from scrap plywood. Tape holds the pad in place while you tighten the clamp so you don't need three hands.

▶ DO IT RIGHT

It may look funky, but a heavy weight, such as a concrete block, is a fast and economical way to clamp the cleats and nailers to the tiles while the adhesive dries. Use a piece of scrap plywood to distribute the weight evenly, but be careful that nothing slips after you apply the pressure or you'll have some undoing to do.

Building the Cube

1 **CUT THE CLEATS.** Begin by cutting the corner cleats from the baluster $\frac{1}{16}$ in. shy of the tile length. Hold off on cutting the top and bottom nailers because their measures will be taken after the corner cleats have been glued to the tiles. (See the drawing on p. 35 for cleat positions.)

2 **GO CLAMPING.** Use a caulking gun to apply two $\frac{1}{4}$-in. beads of construction adhesive along one edge of a corner cleat. Then press the cleat flush to the tile's edge and hold it there with a couple of clamps. For now, just glue the four corner cleats to two tiles, then take a break.

3 **CREATE THE CUBE.** Glue the two cleated sides to the two cleatless tiles. Once again, carefully align the cleat edges flush with the tile edges. You can tape the sides in place while the adhesive dries, but spring clamps will make alignment a lot easier. Use a framing square to check that the cube is square. Allow the assembly to dry.

4 **ADD TOP & BOTTOM NAILERS.** Measure for top and bottom nailers. Aim for a snug—but not tight—fit. Cut the nailers, then glue and clamp them in place.

Adding the Trim

5 **CUT THE FRAMES.** While the nailer-to-tile joints are drying, mark cut lines for the trim-frame miter joints with a combination square. Then make the cuts. Remember to make all cuts to the waste side of your cut line.

6 **ASSEMBLE THE TRIM FRAMES.** Apply construction adhesive to the mitered board ends. Then nail joints together with 1½-in. brads, two per joint, to hold them in position while the adhesive dries. Clamp the trim frame members to your worktable to keep them from slipping while you hammer in the brads. Or use miter clamps to hold the joints until the adhesive dries. Next, cut corner molding to the length of the tile, less ¹⁄₁₆ in. Then stain the assembled frames and corner molding with a foam brush.

7 **ATTACH THE FRAMES.** Set the assembly on top of the top frame and check to be sure it's centered. An equal amount of the top trim frame should show on all sides. Then drive 1⅝-in. exterior screws through the underside of the nailers to attach the trim frame. You will need to drive the screws at a slight angle in order to allow clearance for the drill. Turn the assembly over and do the same to attach the bottom trim frame.

8 **INSTALL CORNER TRIM, CASTERS & SLATS.** Apply adhesive to the corner molding and secure all four corners with tape. Install four ball-type casters at each corner. Then cut the bottom slats slightly shorter than the inside dimension of the planter, and lay them on top of the bottom nailers. Space the slats about ¼ in. apart for drainage. There's no need to fasten them to the nailers.

5 6

7 8

The subtle texture of tile adds another dimension to a plant-filled container.

Tile isn't just for the floor! Create a dynamic display piece by combining the beauty of tile with plants. Use the colors and textures of tile, as well as paint, to complement the intended plant or to create a container that's a focal point in itself. Small mosaic tiles or a mix of tiles of different sizes also make eye-catching designs. If you use different size tiles, you'll need to first adhere them to a piece of wood cut to the size of your container.

This indoor version of the roll-around planter was made with 6-in. by 6-in. tiles and finished with off-the-shelf trim. It's light-weight enough that casters aren't needed.

The subtle colors of the tile and trim used in this planter let the plants take center stage. Casters allow the planter to be relocated for the best outdoor growing conditions.

Fruit at Your Fingertips

Grow your own STRAWBERRIES & HERBS in these attractive planters

EVEN IF YOU DON'T HAVE A YARD you can still have a garden. With this strawberry planter, you can grow fresh, fragrant berries or create an herb garden. Either way, you'll get the bounty and satisfaction of homegrown produce. And if you're a busy—or an inexperienced—gardener, you'll appreciate our tips for keeping your plants healthy, tasty, and low maintenance. When summer is over, you can bring the outdoors in by growing a mini herb garden on your kitchen windowsill in a set of planters with matching drip tray.

| ADD A WATER SOURCE | PLANT STRAWBERRIES | PLANT HERBS | FINISH UP |

▶ **DO IT RIGHT**

To minimize root damage, cut individual plants from the packs they come in using a pair of sturdy scissors. Plants with trimmed roots are less susceptible to transplant shock, wilting, and disease, and they will grow and bear fruit more quickly.

⬝ LINGO

Resin-coated fertilizer pellets, also called slow-release fertilizers, nourish plants according to their needs during an entire growing season. The pellets release nutrients slowly with each watering.

Tools & Gear

You'll need your household repair tools and your gardening tote on hand for these projects—and you'll also be visiting the kitchen-gadget drawer for a few things.

HAMMER. A standard 16-oz. carpenter's hammer will do.

SCREWDRIVER OR ICE PICK. You'll need a screwdriver or an old-fashioned ice pick to use with the hammer for poking holes in the plastic water bottle.

SCOOPS. You'll want a large metal or plastic scoop for filling the potting containers with soil. Get a smaller one for pouring soil into gaps between tightly packed plants.

PRUNING SHEARS. A small pair of pruners is handy for removing damaged stems and strawberries.

SCISSORS. A durable pair of scissors will serve you in good stead for trimming moss and cutting strawberry plants apart.

WATERING CAN OR HOSE. You'll need a watering can or hose that can supply a small, slow stream of water for filling the reservoir in the strawberry jar and for gently watering the soil around herb plants.

COOL TOOL

Standard pruners bruise delicate stems. The garnishes you cut with them will be unsightly, and the plants will have damaged and disease-susceptible stems. Keep a collection of sharp snippers handy for garden work. The best ones are bypass shears, which have two sharp blades. Get blades that are dishwasher-safe stainless steel. Pictured here (counter-7clockwise from top) are lightweight pruners, serrated kitchen shears that pop apart for easy cleaning, and small craft scissors.

What to Buy

1| BOTTLE OF WATER. Freeze it, poke holes in it, and put it into the soil (without its cap), and it becomes a nearly invisible reservoir for watering a strawberry jar. The holes are easier to poke if the water is frozen—if it's not frozen, you'll get soaked.

2| PLANTERS. Terra-cotta pots, planters, and strawberry jars work well for these projects.

3| ROCKS. The robust plants in these projects need maximum root room, so instead of using a layer of gravel for drainage, simply place one small rock over each drain hole in the containers to keep soil from sifting out.

4| POTTING SOIL. Look for packaged potting mixes containing soil or compost. Avoid soilless mixes made of peat moss because once they dry out, they are very hard to rehydrate.

5| PERLITE. Herbs and strawberries grow best in well-drained soil. To increase drainage without adding weight to the planter, blend two-thirds soil with one-third perlite.

6| PLANTS. You can choose from three types of strawberry plants: June-bearing, day neutral, or everbearing. The June-bearing varieties produce a heavy crop in early summer. Day neutral and everbearing plants produce lighter crops of berries throughout the growing season. The best herbs for potting have the words "bush" or "compact" in their names, or are naturally small plants like parsley, cilantro, thyme, and oregano.

7| NEWSPAPER. Newspaper protects work surfaces and also makes a biodegradable wrap for plant roots to protect them as you push them into the pockets of a strawberry jar.

8| SLOW-RELEASE FERTILIZER. This type of fertilizer releases nutrients slowly with each watering, nourishing plants for an entire growing season.

9| SHEET MOSS. You'll use this to plug the openings around the plants in a strawberry jar so that soil is not washed out of the pockets with watering.

10| GRAVEL. Aquarium gravel sold at pet shops makes a decorative mulch for potted herbs. Brown gravel looks best with terra-cotta planters.

11| PLANT LABELS. A small plant label for each plant in your potted garden will help you keep track of what you planted.

① NEED A HAND?

Unruly root balls make it hard to insert plants into the pockets of a strawberry jar. To tame root balls, wrap them in newspaper and twist the ends closed before planting. The paper protects the roots and also keeps you from muddying the outside of the jar. Once the paper's in place, forget about it. There's no need to remove and discard the biodegradable paper.

Planting a Strawberry Jar

1 **PUNCH HOLES.** Lay a bottle of frozen water on a folded towel to keep it from rolling, and use a hammer and ice pick or screwdriver to punch holes randomly around the bottle from top to bottom. Set the bottle aside to drain.

2 **FILL IT UP.** Cover the planter's drain hole with a rock to keep soil from sifting out. Combine the soil mix with the perlite. Scoop soil into the jar until it is even with the bottom of the lowest row of holes. Wrap the strawberry plants in newspaper (see NEED A HAND? at left), then insert one plant into each hole in the bottom row, laying the root bundle flat on the soil.

3 **PUT THE BOTTLE IN.** Place the perforated water bottle upright on the soil, centering it in the jar. Hold it steady while you scoop soil around it to reach the bottom of the second row of holes. Now scatter a handful of slow-release fertilizer pellets over the soil, and plant the holes as described in step 2. Add soil until you reach the top row of holes, add fertilizer, and plant as before.

4 **FINISH UP.** Scoop soil into the jar to about 1 in. below the jar's rim. (The neck of the bottle should be visible for easy watering.) Add enough plants to fill the top of the pot, fill gaps between them with soil, and firm the soil with your fingers. Next, tuck some moss between the plants in the pockets

and between the plants in the top of the jar. Pour water gently into the pot around the bottle to moisten it, then fill the bottle with water. Remember to fill the bottle with each watering. Trim off any damaged strawberries and your planter is done.

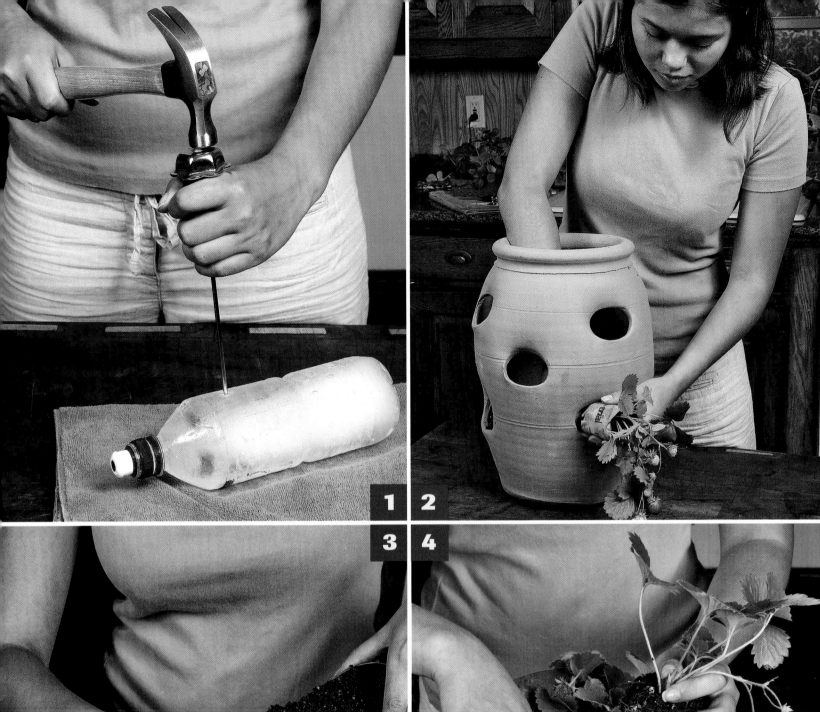

✳ DO IT FAST

Don't allow herbs to flower. Herbs lose flavor when they flower and set seed. To prolong their useful life, be vigilant about trimming off buds and flowers. The trimmings make tasty garnishes for salads, entrees, and iced tea.

Making an Herb Planter

5 **COVER THE DRAIN HOLE.** Place a rock over each drain hole in the container. A rock will fit loosely enough to allow excess water to drain out, but it will keep soil from washing out of the planter with each watering.

6 **ADD SOIL & FERTILIZER.** Mix the perlite with the potting soil. Scoop the potting mix directly over the rocks covering the drain holes. Fill the container high enough so that when you set the root balls of the herbs on the potting mix, the base of the plants will be about ½ in. below the soil's rim. Next, sprinkle a handful of slow-release fertilizer over the potting mix in the container.

7 **SET PLANTS INTO THE CONTAINER.** Unpot each herb plant and set its root ball on the fertilized layer of soil in the container. If roots are thickly entwined when you unpot, gently pull the outer roots apart before positioning the root ball. The goal is to pack plants side by side, so that you can plant a wider variety. Fill all the gaps between plants with potting medium, and press it in place with your fingers.

8 **MULCH, LABEL & WATER.** When all the plants are in place, cover the soil with a layer of decorative-gravel mulch that's just thick enough to reach the rim of the pot. Identify each herb with a plant label. Water the soil gently until water runs from the drain holes.

5

6

7

8

Decorative strawberry jars like these ceramic pots add an elegant touch.

Once you've mastered the potting techniques for these projects, it's time to exercise artistic license with the variety of plants and containers available. If space is at a premium, you can pack an herb garden into a strawberry jar, growing one herb per "pocket." These jars come in a variety of materials and sizes—if you choose a small one, skip the water-bottle reservoir because your plants will need all the root room they can get.

Square planters are ideal for individual plants, such as shrubby rosemary and bay trees, while long planters and strawberry pots can accommodate a collection of smaller herbs or strawberries.

This plastic turntable with a non-slip surface makes light work of turning heavy planters, so that you can plant along the back edges or reach the back pockets of a strawberry planter. You'll find turntables in the kitchen department of a department store or in stores that sell kitchen gadgets.

Brighten your kitchen windowsill and spice up your winter meals with the fresh flavor of herbs grown in a windowsill-planter set complete with its own drip tray.

Group herb-filled containers together for an eclectic mini herb garden.

Strawberry jars aren't just for strawberries. For a space-saving herb garden, put one herb in each pocket of a strawberry jar. This container includes salvia, oregano, winter savory, golden lemon thyme, silver thyme, rosemary, Vietnamese coriander, tricolor sage, and French tarragon.

Earthly Delights

Build a **HYPERTUFA PLANTER** that mimics real stone

HYPERTUFA, A GREAT SYNTHETIC substitute for tufa rock, can be used to make all sorts of things. The process and recipe for making hypertufa are simple—simple enough that you can make your own, as shown in this project. A good hypertufa should look like its real counterpart—rough, hand-hewn, and earthy. The great thing about making your own container is that you can create just about any shape and size you want. The real tufa planters featured at the end of the project will provide inspiration for making your own hypertufa.

MOUND   MIX   COVER   SHAPE

⊛ WHAT'S DIFFERENT?

Many people use the terms concrete and cement interchangeably, but there is a difference. Concrete is actually made with cement (as well as with sand and gravel). For your hypertufa, you will be making a kind of lightweight concrete using cement to bind perlite and peat moss together. Make sure you purchase Portland cement rather than one of the premixed concrete mixes.

✳ DO IT NOW

Before you start mixing the ingredients, sift the peat moss, and set it aside. That way it's ready when it's time to mix the concrete ingredients.

Tools & Gear

This project will use more tools from your garden shed than from your carpenter's toolbox. You'll need the following:

WHEELBARROW. You can mix the hypertufa ingredients in your wheelbarrow, or buy a large plastic tub.

HOE. Think of this as a swizzle stick for the cement mixture. If you're going to buy one, consider getting a mason's hoe, which has two holes through the blade that make mixing easier. A regular garden hoe works nearly as well.

SHOVEL. You'll need one to measure out the ingredients and to pile up the dirt mold.

SMALL MASON'S TROWEL. You'll use this to smooth and shape both the mold and the outside of the planter.

SAFETY GOGGLES. Getting cement dust in your eyes is excruciatingly painful, not to mention dangerous.

DUST MASK. You don't want to breathe cement or perlite dust.

HEAVY-DUTY LATEX GLOVES. Cement mixes are caustic and will cause your skin to peel. Wear gloves to protect yourself if your hands will touch the cement.

WIRE BRUSH. A few brushstrokes add character.

SOIL SIEVE. You need to sift out any clumps and debris from the peat moss. You can buy a sieve or make one yourself (see COOL TOOL below).

COOL TOOL

You can make your own soil sieve. Screw together a simple frame of 1×3s or 1×4s with drywall or decking screws. Then use fencing staples to attach a piece of 1/4-in. mesh hardware cloth. Make your frame wide enough to span your wheelbarrow to make it easier to use.

What to Buy

Most of the materials you'll need to make a hypertufa are available at your local home center, hardware store, or lumberyard.

1| PORTLAND CEMENT. It usually comes in 94-lb. sacks, which is enough to make several planters.

2| PERLITE. This lightweight soil additive is mixed with the cement.

3| PEAT MOSS. You'll mix the peat moss with the cement and perlite. Put it through a sieve before mixing to eliminate clumps and twigs.

4| FIBERMESH. This is a form of chopped fiber (either fiberglass or plastic) that you add to the hypertufa mix to make it stronger. Although it's used in some concrete mixes, it may be more difficult to find than the other ingredients. Try your local masonry supply store or look on the Internet. (Nycon®, Inc., has a product called Control 1000 that it sells in small quantities.)

5| WATER. You might need a little water to keep the mix moist as you work it.

6| PLASTIC TRASH BAGS OR SHEETING. Hypertufa mix is sticky, so you'll want to put it on plastic for mixing and working to make cleanup easier. You'll also use the plastic to cover the planter to keep it from drying out too fast and cracking.

THE RECIPE

Recipes for small quantities of concrete are usually specified by proportion—so many units of cement to so many units of sand to so many units of gravel, and so on. A good hypertufa mix is 2 parts Portland cement, 3 parts peat moss, 3 parts perlite, and a handful of fibermesh.

To make a hypertufa mix for the planter shown in this project, mix together the following:

4 shovels Portland cement
6 shovels sifted peat moss
6 shovels perlite
2 handfuls fibermesh

The above recipe yields enough to make a medium-size planter—roughly 15 in. long by 12 in. wide by 9 in. deep.

Making the Planter

1 **MAKE THE MOLD.** Mound up a pile of soil on a sheet of plastic. Wet it if necessary so it sticks together and holds its shape. Sculpt it with your trowel to form the shape you want on the inside of your planter. Cover the mold with plastic to keep the cement mix from stick-

ing to the soil. The plastic will also keep the soil from wicking the moisture out of the cement mix too quickly, causing cracks.

2 **MIX THE INGREDIENTS.** Put on your goggles and dust mask. Following the recipe on p. 55, scoop the cement, perlite, peat moss, and fibermesh into your wheelbarrow or bucket and mix thoroughly. Add water a little at a time until the mix is wet but not soupy. You've added enough

water when you can squeeze a handful of mix and the resulting clump retains the imprint of your hand. Wear gloves when you handle the mix.

3 **CAST THE PLANTER.** Apply the mix to the mold until it's 1½ in. to 2 in. thick. You can use your trowel or even your hands to pack the mix over the mold (wear your gloves). If the mix sags, place bricks or pavers around the edges to help keep the mix in place, but remove them after a couple of hours or they will stick to the hypertufa mix. Sculpt the

planter to whatever shape you like with the trowel. As a final step, push a small stick through the bottom a couple of times to make drainage holes. Cover the planter with plastic to allow it to cure slowly.

4 **FINISH THE PLANTER.** Allow the planter to cure in a shady location for 15 hours to 48 hours, depending on the size and the weather. Check it periodically. When the edge of your trowel can scratch the surface, the planter has cured to the point where it can be uncovered and removed from the mold. Go over the surface with a wire brush to give your planter a weathered look. Let the planter sit for another 3 to 4 weeks to finish curing.

This low-to-the-ground, oval-shape container is well suited to the free-form method of making a hypertufa.

Hypertufa was created as a replacement for tufa (pronounced like tuba) rock, a soft, spongy material that was used centuries ago to make tubs, pots, and planters. Eye-catching hypertufa containers are stylish and durable—they'll survive the elements and look great through the years.

A grouping of several tufa pots is an easy way to create the look of a rock garden.

This tufa box planter bears the scratch marks of the tools used to carve it.

Rectangular or round, high or low, you can try countless shapes and configurations.

Hanging Gardens

This classic MOSS-LINED BASKET is a living bouquet

NOTHING SAYS "WELCOME" like a hanging basket brimming with colorful flowers. These go-anywhere gardens add beauty and motion to a balcony, entrance, or patio, and brighten up empty walls and fences. This wire basket creation is lined with richly textured moss, and flowers and greenery spill from the sides for an incomparably lush effect. And what's more, the moisture-retaining plastic insert makes this a basket that's as easy to care for as it is on the eyes.

LINE WITH MOSS   PROTECT WITH PLASTIC   PLANT   HANG & TRIM

A moisture gauge gives you an instant and accurate reading of soil moisture. Insert the probe 4 in. into the hanging basket and check the gauge. If the needle rests in the green (moist) zone or in the blue (wet) zone, no water is needed. If it swings toward the red (dry) zone, it's time to water.

Moisture-retaining crystals reduce upkeep and plant stress. When mixed into potting soil, they absorb moisture with each watering and release it slowly to plant roots, which means you water less often.

Tools & Gear

You are likely to have some of the tools you'll need for this project in your gardening tote.

SCISSORS. A durable pair of scissors will serve you in good stead for trimming and shaping the moss and the plastic liner of this basket. They're also handy for removing faded flowers.

UTILITY KNIFE. This sharp tool, also called a razor knife, makes short work of slicing holes in the side of a basket liner so that you can insert plants. When cutting tough cocoa-fiber liner, you'll want to change blades between cuts.

SCOOPS. You'll want a large scoop for filling the basket with soil before planting, and a smaller one for pouring soil into gaps between tightly packed plants.

NEWSPAPER. You'll wrap the roots in newspaper before planting to help protect them.

PRUNING SHEARS. A small pair of pruners is handy for removing damaged stems and for shaping plants after the basket is planted.

WATERING CAN. To keep from dislodging soil and freshly situated plants, you'll want to water the finished basket with a watering can fitted with a "rose." You can also use a hose fitted with a watering wand or a water-breaker nozzle.

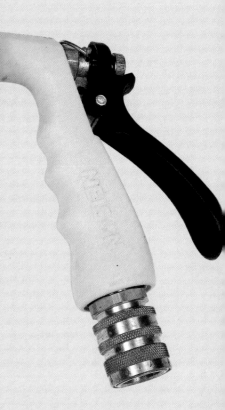

What to Buy

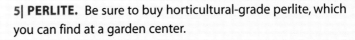

1| MOSS. You want Spanish or sheet moss or a preformed cocoa liner. You can buy gray or tan dried moss or even moss that is dyed a pleasing light green. A bag that is approximately the same diameter as your hanging basket should hold enough to line the basket and decorate the top.

2| WIRE HANGING BASKET. Baskets usually come prepackaged with a chain and hook. Some even include a cocoa liner. Baskets are available in various sizes. The bigger the basket, the more root room and healthier the plants—but bigger baskets are also heavier. A good size is 14 in. in diameter or larger.

3| CLEAR PLASTIC SHEET. You'll need a piece of flexible clear plastic large enough to line the basket and drape over the edges. You'll trim off the excess plastic after planting.

4| POTTING SOIL. Buy enough potting soil to fill the basket. To determine how much you need, set a bag of soil into your chosen empty basket. You want enough soil to fill the basket. Avoid soilless mixes made from peat moss because it dries out too quickly in a basket.

5| PERLITE. Be sure to buy horticultural-grade perlite, which you can find at a garden center.

6| SLOW-RELEASE FERTILIZER. Mix a generous handful of resin-coated fertilizer pellets into the soil before planting to reduce maintenance. They release nutrients slowly with each watering, feeding plants for an entire growing season.

7| WATER-ABSORBING CRYSTALS. Mixing some of these absorbent crystals into the soil before planting will help keep plants from wilting and will keep soil moist longer, easing your watering chores. Be sure to soak the crystals before mixing them into the soil so they don't push soil out of the basket as they expand.

8| PLANTS. For a colorful and richly textured basket, you'll want to buy a variety of flowering and trailing plants. The planter made for this project uses the following plants (shown clockwise from top left in the photo at left): sweet potato vine, ageratum, sweet alyssum, polka dot plant, impatiens, dusty miller, caladium, Swedish ivy, spiky dracaena, iboa vine. You can also fill your basket with culinary herbs or with a combination of pepper and cherry tomato plants.

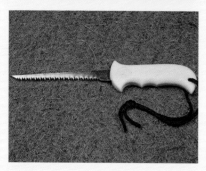

Take a shortcut to a mature-looking basket. Unpot a small hanging basket of mature trailing plants. Cut the root ball and plants into two sections. A transplanting saw cuts quickly through the root ball, dividing it with minimal damage. Place each section against opposite edges of your new hanging basket, and fill in around them with plants of your choice.

➕ WHAT CAN GO WRONG

Is the chain too long? Most hanging baskets come with a set of three chains and a hook for hanging. If the chains are too long, shorten them by removing links with needlenose pliers. Remove as many links as you want until the chain is just the right length.

Building the Basket

1 **LINE THE BASKET WITH MOSS.** Working up from the base of the basket, tuck clumps of moss between the wires so that about ½ in. protrudes. Cover the basket completely, leaving no gaps. Don't worry about neatness; you'll trim the moss later.

2 **LINE THE BASKET WITH PLASTIC.** Cut a sheet of plastic to line the basket, allowing for extra to hang over the rim. This handy "bib" will keep soil off the moss as you plant (after planting, you'll trim it so you don't see it). Push the liner into the basket. Using scissors, poke a drain hole through the plastic at the bottom of the basket. Then measure half way up from the bottom. Using your utility knife, cut four evenly spaced slits (each 3 in. long) around the basket to make holes for shorter-trailing plants. Be sure to cut through the plastic and moss.

3 **PLANT THE BASKET.** Mix together the potting soil, perlite, fertilizer, and water-absorbing crystals. Scoop the soil mixture into the basket to the level of the slits. Wrap the plant roots in pieces of newspaper, twisting the paper closed at the end. Work each root bundle

through a slit in the liner and lay it on the soil (leave the paper on). Next, scoop in enough soil to come to about 1 in. below the rim. First plant trailing plants against the rim of the basket, then set a tall accent plant in the center. Fill the spaces in between with plants of medium height. Pack plants tightly for a lush effect. Firm the soil around the plants as you go.

4 **FINISH UP.** Fill gaps between the plants with soil, pressing it firmly in place with your fingers. Cover bare patches with moss, then trim away the plastic bib. Attach the chains and hook and hang the basket up for final inspection. Turn it slowly, trim off unruly strands of moss and damaged stems, then water gently.

While a variety of plant shapes and colors can heighten visual interest, stick to a couple of different plants and repeat them throughout the container.

Grapevines were woven into an artful, rustic hanging basket. The red and pink color palette of the basket flowers works well with the colors of the perennials close by.

Let your imagination be your guide

as you create your hanging garden. Hanging baskets are portable, so use them to brighten up a bare spot in your home or yard. Use plants that play off existing colors in your decor if you want your garden to blend or create a dramatic splash by featuring plants that make a statement. You can't go wrong with whatever you choose.

Hanging plants can add color and interest anywhere—even on an arbor. This basket helps to soften the hard lines of the wood structure.

A shepherd's hook with multiple arms lets you hang several planters.

Pots come in an endless array of shapes, sizes, and colors. Mix and match to your plants and surrounding space—whether inside or out.

67

Easy Embellished Pots

Turn ordinary clay pots into distinctive planters with TILE, SHELLS, or PAINT

SOMETIMES ORDINARY JUST WON'T DO! A clay pot is the perfect beginning to a personalized planter. Besides embellishing pots with tile, broken dishes, bits of jewelry or stained glass, and even computer chips make colorful mosaic materials. In the pages that follow you'll find three easy techniques for creating your own work of art. One technique uses small tiles to create a mosaic; another uses shells to create a cottage look. The last project creates an antique look with a crackle finish. There's something here for everyone.

START WITH TILES . . .   **OR TRY SHELLS**   **GROUT**   **TRY PAINT, TOO**

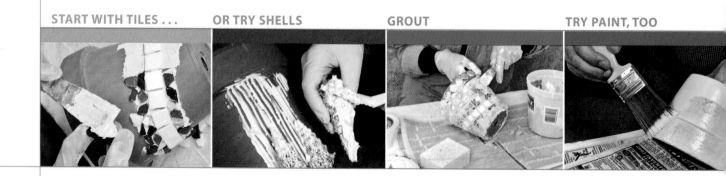

✚ SAFETY FIRST

The lime in grout will cause skin to peel. Wear latex gloves as protection. If you do get grout on your hands, wash them and then rinse with lemon juice or vinegar.

▶ DO IT RIGHT

Contrasting or complementary color? For a cohesive, sophisticated look, choose a complementary grout color—one similar to the colors of the tiles or shells. For drama, use contrasting grout to make the pieces stand out.

Tools & Gear

A few tools, a few art supplies, and a few tile-setting products are all you need to transform a pot into a planter.

PUTTY KNIFE. Use your putty knife to mix the tile adhesive and then spread it.

PAINT BUCKET. These plastic containers, available wherever paint is sold, are handy for mixing powder-type adhesives and grout. You'll also want to have a bucket of clean water handy for cleaning your tools and hands when you're applying grout.

NOTCHED TROWEL OR PAINT COMB. A notched trowel, which is designed to spread tile mastic, may be too unwieldy to use on a small flowerpot. If so, substitute a flexible, smaller paint comb made for faux paint application.

PAINTBRUSHES. Use 2-in.- or 3-in.-wide bristle or foam brushes to apply paint. You'll want a smaller brush to put on sealer.

COOL TOOL

Professional tile installers use metal trowels to work grout into the joints of tiled floors and walls, but you'll need something smaller and more flexible for flowerpots. Inexpensive, flexible plastic artists' palette knives from your local art store are perfect for working grout into the spaces between seashells or tiles.

What to Buy

All of the projects start with a clean terra-cotta pot. But then you'll need different materials depending on which project you choose.

TILE MOSAIC & SEASHELL POTS

1| TILE ADHESIVE. This thick, sticky bonding material is used to hold down tiles and other decorative elements.

2| TILE/MOSAIC PIECES/SEASHELLS. You can buy small tiles at craft-supply stores, or collect and break up your own pieces. Shells up to 1 in. long are easiest to fit around a flowerpot. Smaller shells work well on the rim.

3| DUST MASK. Wear a mask to minimize exposure to grout dust and shards of cut mosaics.

4| RUBBER GLOVES. Disposable gloves protect hands against cuts, stains, abrasion, and caustic grout.

5| GROUT. Use fine-textured, unsanded powdered grout for mosaic projects. You can buy white or colored grout. If you'd like custom colors, buy tinted grout or mix acrylic paints thinned with water into white grout.

6| SPONGE & TOWEL. Use a damp sponge or cloth to wipe away excess grout. Use a dry terry-cloth towel to polish the finished piece after the grout dries.

7| TILE/GROUT SEALER. A sealer, while not technically necessary, will prevent stains and keep your pot looking nice longer.

8| ACRYLIC ADDITIVE. Instead of mixing grout with water, mix it with this liquid additive to make mosaic flowerpots waterproof.

9| PALETTE KNIVES. These small tools make applying grout easy (see COOL TOOL, facing page).

10| COTTON SWABS. Use a dampened cotton swab to wipe excess grout from crevices.

11| SPRAY BOTTLE. Spray water to keep grout moist as you work.

CRACKLE-PAINT POT

1| ACRYLIC PRIMER. Prime with acrylic primer before painting.

2| PAPER. Line the interior of the pot with paper to keep it clean when spraying the exterior with paint.

3| PAINTER'S TAPE. Tape off the rim of the pot before applying decorative coatings to keep the edge and interior clean.

4| ACRYLIC PAINT. Use water-based acrylic paint. You want a satin gloss.

5| CLEAR CRACKLE MEDIUM. You can find small amounts at craft stores and larger amounts at paint and home centers. Be sure to read the label to make sure it's compatible with the paint you're using.

6| SPRAY VARNISH. Seal projects with acrylic satin-gloss spray varnish to waterproof and protect the finish against chipping.

7| SANDPAPER. Sand lightly with 220-grit sandpaper between varnish coats.

Tile Mosaic Pot

1 **PLAN YOUR DESIGN.** Pencil a design on paper or directly on the pot. In this case, all that was required was to draw a pair of undulating parallel lines to guide the placement of white mosaic tiles, which would be edged with colorful pieces of sea glass before applying a field of blue tiles.

2 **APPLY ADHESIVE & TILES.** Use a putty knife to mix up a small batch of tile adhesive in a plastic paint bucket. Then put on your gloves and spread a thin layer of adhesive over a small area on the pot. Begin applying tile and mosaic pieces. For good adhesion, spread a little adhesive on the back of each piece before pressing it in place. Follow the design you drew in step 1. Allow the pot to dry overnight.

3 **APPLY GROUT.** Mix up enough grout for the entire pot. It should be the consistency of toothpaste. Spread the grout over the surface of the tiles. Don't worry—this step is meant to be messy. You can apply the grout with your hands or with a putty knife. Use a damp sponge to force the grout between pieces and remove excess from the face of the tiles.

4 **CLEAN & SEAL.** Wait a few minutes so that the grout has time to dry slightly. Then use a clean, damp sponge to remove all grout from the face of the tiles. Later, when the grout is dry, polish off any grout haze with a soft, dry towel, and brush on a coat of sealer.

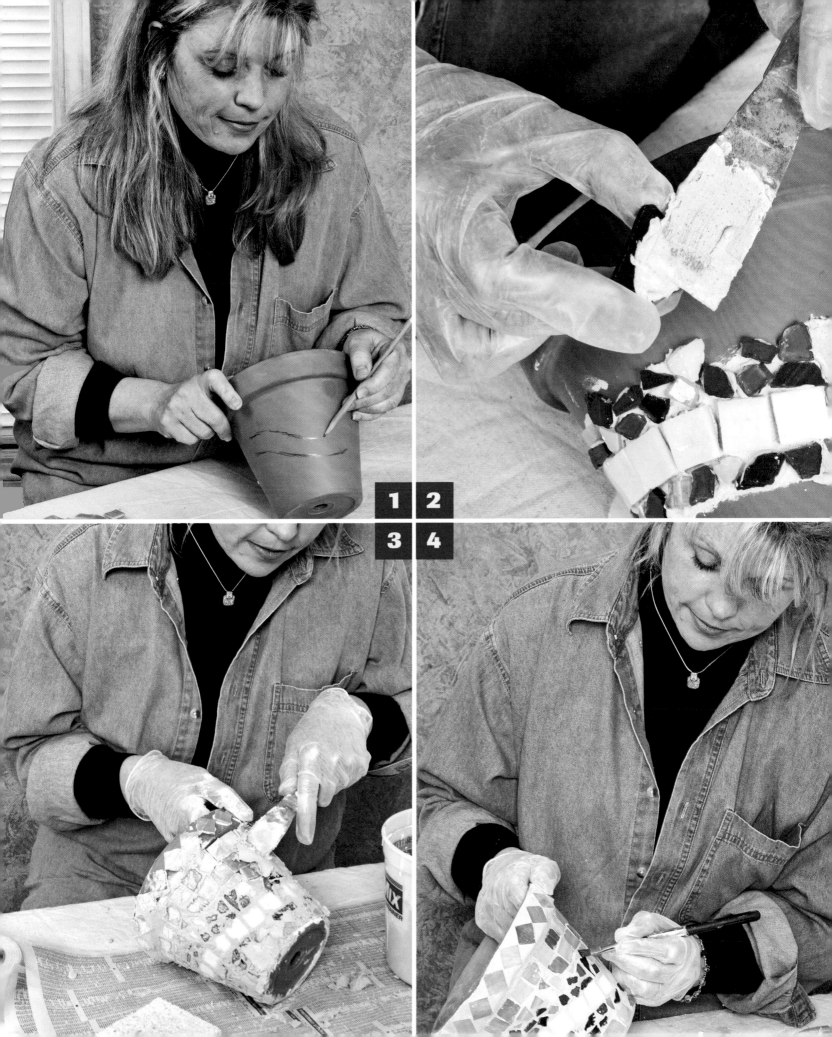

Sometimes grout or adhesive dries where you don't want it. Scrape it away with a knife.

▶ **DO IT RIGHT**

A dry clay pot can quickly absorb water in the adhesive, making the adhesive dry out too quickly. To give yourself more working time, lightly mist the pot with water before you apply adhesive.

Shell Mosaic

1 **SPREAD ADHESIVE ON THE POT.** Using a notched trowel or paint comb, spread tile adhesive from the rim of the pot to about ¼ in. from the base. Apply adhesive to one small area at a time.

2 **APPLY THE SHELLS.** Working from the bottom to the top, create tight, uniform spacing to minimize the amount of grout you'll need later. Butter each large shell with a little adhesive on the back, then press it firmly into the adhesive already on the pot. When the shells fill the area you've covered with adhesive, apply additional patches of adhesive and shells until the pot is covered below the rim. Cover the rim last, using smaller shells. Set the completed pot in an airy place and allow the adhesive to dry overnight.

3 **MIX & APPLY GROUT.** Mix grout according to package directions, but substitute acrylic additive for water to make your project water resistant. You want the grout to be the consistency of toothpaste. Work the grout carefully between the shells with a palette knife. Press and smooth the grout with your fingers as you go. You'll have about an hour to work before the grout hardens, so mix small batches and spray occasionally with water to keep the grout from drying too fast. As you work, wipe excess grout off the shells with a cotton swab and wipe the pot with a damp cloth to get rid of extra grout and any haze.

4 **GIVE THE POT A FINISHED LOOK.** If grout has cracked while drying, apply more. If there's any haze that you missed while working, wipe it off as soon as the grout is firm. If you wait until it is thoroughly dry, the haze may not come off. Allow at least an hour for

the grout to dry completely, and then polish the shells with a dry rag. Waterproof the interior by coating the inside of the pot with acrylic sealer. The pot is now ready to use.

1   **2**

3   **4**

Achieve the crackle effect you want by varying your brush technique and the thickness of your top coat of paint. The cracks will follow the direction of the brush strokes. For parallel cracks, lay down brush strokes in only one direction. To create a checkered pattern, overlap strokes that run at 90 degrees to each other. To create large cracks, use thick paint; thin the paint to get smaller cracks.

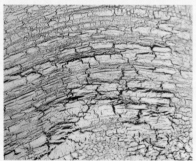

Paint in 60° F to 80° F weather. Temperatures that are too hot or too cold change drying times and may prevent crackling or leave you with a sticky mess.

Crackle Paint

1 **PREP THE POT.** Before you start painting, line the inside of the pot with a piece of paper and tape it to the rim of the pot. Coat the pot's exterior with primer, and allow it to dry according to package directions.

2 **APPLY THE BASE COAT.** Brush or spray one or two base coats of acrylic paint over the primer until the color is uniform. Allow the base coat to dry according to package directions.

3 **APPLY THE CRACKLE MEDIUM.** Brush on the crackle medium, keeping the brush saturated. Don't try to brush out the crackle medium to smooth the coat—it ruins the crackle effect. Allow the medium to dry overnight.

4 **APPLY A TOP COAT.** Use a clean brush or foam applicator to apply the top coat of paint. The cracks will begin to appear as soon as you lay down paint. Don't rework the paint, or you will ruin the effect. Allow the paint to dry for about an hour, then carefully remove the paper and tape. Let the pot continue to dry for 48 hours. To seal the finish after it's dried, spray the pot with two coats of acrylic varnish. Follow the directions on the can, sanding lightly between coats. Don't worry about getting varnish on the inside of the pot—it won't show and it provides a bit of extra protection.

Combine a wash of thinned white paint with decoupage to bring a subtlety to the red orange of a terra-cotta pot.

Mosaics can make an ordinary object a piece of garden art. Pamper the birds with a mosaic birdbath.

You can do just about anything to dress up terracotta.

Explore varied and very simple paint and decorating treatments ranging from sponging and dry brushing to decoupage. Flowerpots are a great place to start, but don't stop there. You can embellish birdbaths, saucers, table-tops, plaques, and other items for your own use or to give as gifts.

Mix and match broken tiles and dishes to create your own whimsical patterns.

When it comes to painting pots, the design possibilities are endless. Try a free-hand design or start with a stencil until you're comfortable experimenting on your own.

Old pieces of heirloom china don't have to go in the trash. You can reassemble them in a mosaic to create intricate patterns—and to preserve memories.

Colorful and fun, these mosaic pots liven up the plants—and the outdoors.

On Deck

Keep deck space free & clear with
this **BALCONY BOX** that can be made in an afternoon

THERE'S NOTHING MORE RELAXING THAN sitting on a deck, glass of iced lemonade in hand, surrounded by your favorite plants. This easy-to-build planter can hold an annual garden of brightly colored flowers or a kitchen garden complete with sweet-smelling herbs and vegetables—all without taking up valuable deck space. Build several and create your own garden retreat. Each planter is made from a single piece of 1×10 pine and a couple dozen nails, so it's a low-cost project as well.

CUT THE PIECES   BORE DRAINAGE HOLES   ASSEMBLE THE BOX   APPLY STAIN

✳ DO IT NOW

If you plan to use a liner in your planter, buy the liner first and adjust the dimensions of your box if necessary. You may want to cut holes in the liner to align with the drainage holes in the base of the planter or else your plants may get swamped during the first downpour.

◼ LINGO

You should always cut to the waste side of the line. This means that the inside edge of your blade should just graze the outside edge—or waste side— of your cut line. This helps to ensure accurate cuts and workpieces that are not cut too short!

Tools & Gear

In addition to common shop tools, such as a tape measure, combination square, and hammer, you'll also need:

DRILL/DRIVER & BITS. An electric drill will allow you to quickly predrill nail holes and to bore drainage holes. For the latter you'll need a 1¼-in. spade bit.

CLAMPS. You can never have too many clamps when building a project. You'll be prepared for anything with an assortment of Quick-Grip clamps in various lengths, spring clamps, and C-clamps.

FRAMING SQUARE. A simple and yet amazingly useful tool. Use it to check boards for squareness, to mark cut and drill lines, and as a guide for your jigsaw when making crosscuts.

BLOCK PLANE. Use a plane or sandpaper on a sanding block to cut bevels on all exposed edges. This not only looks neater but will also help prevent splinters.

RANDOM-ORBIT SANDER. Although smooth wood is not of paramount importance with an outdoor planter box, an electric sander will remove stubborn markings and blemishes on the stock.

JIGSAW. Use a jigsaw to make all of the cuts in this project.

What to Buy

1| LUMBER. Select a 1×10 no. 2 board that is not cupped or twisted. Store it in a dry place until you're ready to use it.

2| FASTENERS. Coated ring-shank nails will resist corrosion and hold joints tighter than smooth-shank nails. Their only drawback is that they're tougher to pull out should you make a mistake.

3| WOOD PRESERVATIVE. A couple of coats of preservative will increase the life of your planter by preventing premature rot. Read the label on the can to figure out the drying time.

4| STAIN. A redwood-colored water-based stain was used for this project, but you can use whatever exterior finish you like.

5| SANDPAPER. One sheet of medium-grit sandpaper should be all you need for this project—or one 5-in.-dia. sanding disk if you're using a random-orbit sander.

6| DUST MASK. You should wear a dust mask when generating lots of sawdust during cutting or sanding.

7| ROLLER OR PAINTBRUSH. Use a roller or foam brush to apply the wood preservative. A foam brush or a polyester or nylon paintbrush work well for applying the stain.

8| JIGSAW BLADES. Have a variety on hand. The blades for crosscutting and ripping are wide and have fewer teeth per inch. Narrow blades are for cutting curves. Have extras on hand as well. Jigsaw blades dull quickly.

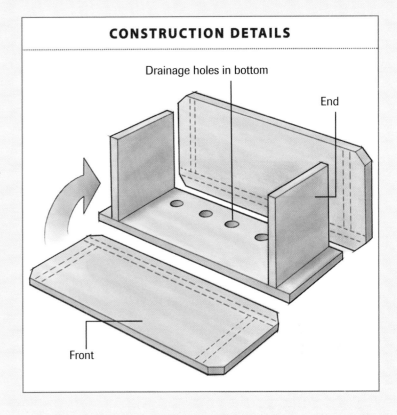

CONSTRUCTION DETAILS

Drainage holes in bottom

End

Front

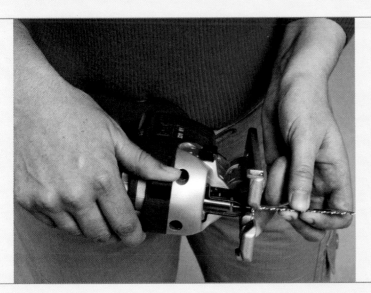

COOL TOOL

A **battery-powered jigsaw** has plenty of power to both rip and crosscut the pieces needed to build the planter. Blade changes are simple with a tool like the one shown here. Simply retract the blade-change lever, insert the blade and release. Chuck a smaller, thin curve-cutting blade when cutting optional inside or outside radius details.

Sometimes, though not often, the ends of boards are not cut square as they come from the lumberyard. Use a framing square to check. If the end is not square, mark a cut line with the square and make a new end cut.

Cutting the Pieces

1 **PREP THE STOCK.** Sand all surfaces to clean up unwanted markings, stains, and other minor blemishes. Use a random-orbit sander to get the job done quickly or use sandpaper and a sanding block. Next, mark all cutting lines (see the drawing on p. 83). Mark an X to the waste side of the line so it's clear which side is waste when you're cutting.

2 **CUT THE SIDES & ENDS.** To ensure straight cuts when making crosscuts or rips, use a guide. To position your guide, you need to know the blade offset (the distance between the inside edge of the blade and the saw show edge). Measure and mark the offset  on your workpiece, and clamp your guide so its edge aligns with the mark. A framing square makes a good guide for most crosscuts. Align the long edge of the square flush to the edge of the board. Use the short edge of the square to guide the saw as you make your cut.

3 **RIP TO WIDTH.** Cut—or rip—the boards to the correct width (see the drawing on p. 83). A straight board makes a good guide or straightedge when making rip cuts that are longer than a framing square. Mark your blade offset as described in step 2. Clamp the straightedge securely in place. When making your cut, be sure to keep the edge of the saw shoe bearing against the guide—or else your saw will wander and your cut will not be straight.

4 **CUT CORNERS.** Using a jigsaw, cut off the four corners on each side. Before you cut, mark a 45-degree cutting line using a combination square. When cutting, be careful not to put your hand under the corner you're cutting.

Speed the process of marking nail positions by measuring the position once and using a square-guided pencil to draw a nailing line. Then go back and mark the 6-in. nailing intervals.

Use a carpenter's pencil or a small square block of wood to help you ensure alignment of workpieces prior to driving the nails. If one piece is misaligned, other joints will be askew as well.

Building the Box

5 **BEVEL & BORE.** Use a block plane or sanding block to chamfer all edges. When chamfering across the grain, use a 45-degree slicing motion away from the board, take off only a little material per stroke, and keep the blade sharp. When you're done chamfering, bore six to eight 1¼-in.-dia. drainage holes in the planter base as close to the sides as possible.

6 **APPLY PRESERVATIVE & BEGIN ASSEMBLY.** Using a foam brush or roller, apply a liberal coat of wood preservative to all sides and edges prior to assembly. Allow the preservative to dry. Predrill nail holes with a ¹⁄₁₆-in.-dia. bit, then fasten the ends to the base with ring-shank nails. To prevent the pieces from slipping as you hammer, clamp a stop to your worktable as shown. A plastic square, clamped as shown, helps you keep things square and aligned.

7 **ASSEMBLE THE SIDES.** Predrill nail holes and fasten the sides to the ends and to the base with ring-shank nails. You may choose to set the nails with a nail punch and fill with exterior-grade filler, but this isn't necessary. The nails are coated and will not corrode or cause staining any time soon.

8 **APPLY STAIN.** Brush on the stain. Water-based stains can be a bit difficult to apply evenly, so work quickly and strive for even coverage. If you pause in the middle, the stain may dry and leave lap marks (dark blotches where two layers of stain overlap).

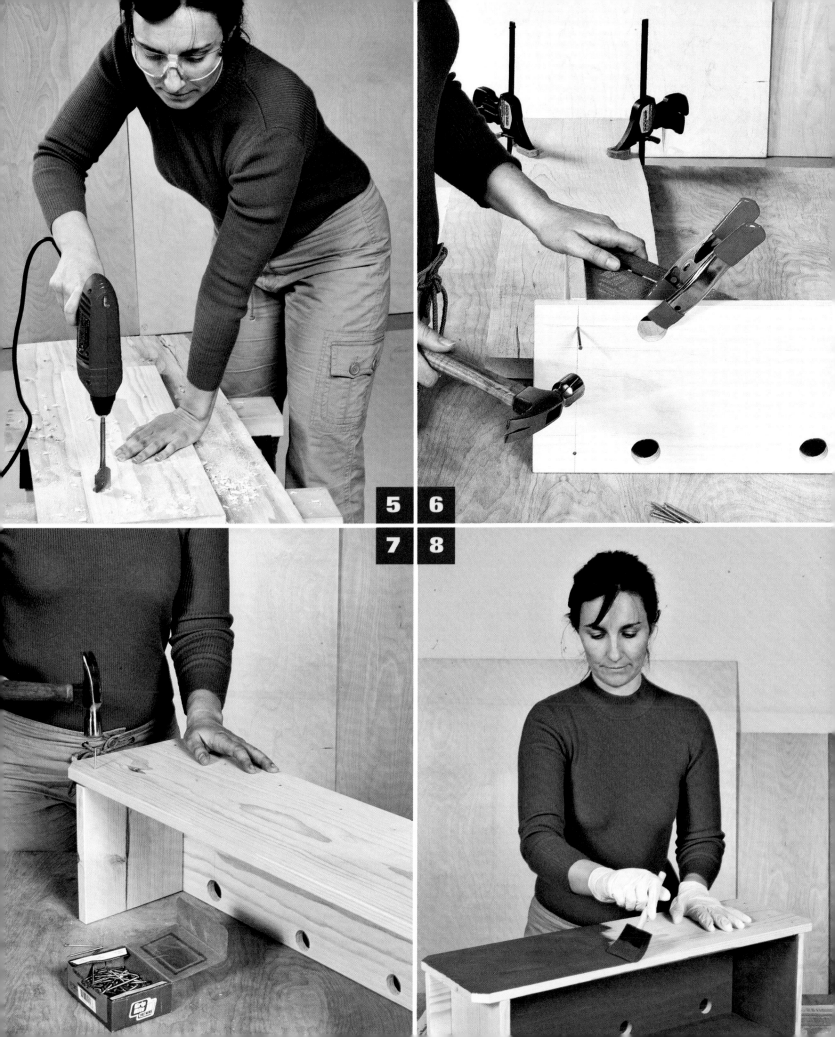

5

6

7

8

A balcony box is perfect for apartment dwellers and homeowners. Changing the color—and plants—is an easy way to garden year-round to reflect the spirit of the seasons.

Get creative with decorative side panel treatments. These were made by first boring holes with a spade bit and then cutting the slots with a straightedge-guided jigsaw.

This colorful balcony box creates a welcoming entry. It's easily viewed from inside the house as well, bringing the feeling of the outdoors in.

The combination of colors in this balcony box gives the effect of a sunset—the perfect backdrop while relaxing on the deck.

Painting is a quick way to change a design. This blue-painted balcony box is a perfect contrast to the pink-purple petunias. In the winter, paint the box white and add red-berried hollies and boughs of pine to brighten a snowy landscape.

Trellis Planter

Give your favorite climbing plants ROOM TO GROW
with this trellis & planter combination.

THERE ARE ANY NUMBER OF climbing plants that will be fun to grow in and on this combination planter/trellis. Clematis, morning glories, roses, even vegetable vines such as cucumbers or runner beans will enjoy a chance to climb their way to the top. Made from plywood, framing lumber, and a vinyl lattice panel, this project is elegant and easy to build. And to make it even easier, this planter is specially designed for already potted plants, so you don't have to plant the box itself. In fact, you may want to build more than one, or adjust the dimensions to suit the space where you can show off the finished project.

CUT THE PLY   MAKE THE TRELLIS   PUT IT TOGETHER   FINISH UP

❖ COOL TOOL

A sliding T-bevel (sometimes called a bevel square) is a layout tool used to transfer angles from one place to another. While a T-bevel doesn't have a built-in angle scale, it can be set to almost any angle from 0 to 180 degrees. Use a protractor (remember that from geometry class?) to lay out the angle on the edge of a scrap. Then set the T-bevel to the angle and draw the angle wherever you need it.

Tools & Gear

To build the trellis and its accompanying planter, you'll need basic tools such as a hammer, string, marker, and tape measure. You'll also need these staples of the carpenter's toolbox:

CIRCULAR SAW. While a jigsaw is more versatile, a circular saw will cut straighter and faster. This is the best tool to use for cutting the plywood panels to size.

DRILL/DRIVER & BITS. You'll need this to predrill holes for the screws and to drive them, too. Make sure you've also got a combination countersink/counterbore bit and a Phillips-head screwdriver bit for your drill.

JIGSAW. If you only own one power saw, this is the one to have. You can use it to make both straight and curved cuts.

COMBINATION SQUARE. Useful for laying out square cuts as well as for measuring.

SLIDING T-BEVEL. You'll need this to mark the angles you'll cut on the planter and trellis frame.

CLAMPS. Clamps are a big help during cutting and screwing because they keep the pieces from moving all over.

SAWHORSES. You'll need these or some other support for cutting long boards.

CHISEL. A basic set ($\frac{1}{4}$ in., $\frac{1}{2}$ in., $\frac{3}{4}$ in., 1 in.) will help you clean up the lap joints used in this project.

MITER SAW. For making exact miter cuts in molding and other small pieces of wood, a miter saw does the trick.

PAINTBRUSH. You'll need a brush for the primer and paint.

PUTTY KNIFE. Use it to apply wood filler to nail and screw holes.

What to Buy

1| EXTERIOR PLYWOOD. To make the planter sides and top, you'll need the better part of a full 4×8 sheet. If you don't have a way to get a full sheet home, most home centers sell partial sheets of plywood, or you can buy a full sheet and have the store cut it for you. Get a good grade, such as A-C or B-C, which has one side that will look nice when painted. Put the rougher C side on the inside of the planter.

2| 2×2s. You'll use these for the trellis frame. You may have to search through the pile to find some straight ones, but it's worth the effort. You'll need three 8-footers.

3| 1×3s. Get two 6-ft. pieces to add a rim to the top of the planter. It's worth extra money to get a better grade of wood.

4| MOLDING. For a finishing touch, get two 6-ft. pieces of molding that will go under the 1×3 rim pieces. The exact profile isn't important—just get something you like.

5| FLOWER POT. The project shown here uses a 16-in.-dia. pot. If you want a much bigger or smaller pot, you'll need to adjust the dimensions of your box.

6| POLYURETHANE GLUE. You'll need this moisture-resistant glue to assemble the project.

7| DECK SCREWS. You'll need about 1 lb. of #8 2-in. screws to assemble the planter. You'll also need a handful of #8 1¼-in. screws to assemble the trellis frame.

8| NAILS. You'll need a handful of 3d finish nails to install the molding. Make sure to get hot-dipped galvanized nails so your fasteners won't rust.

9| SANDPAPER. For a smooth finish you'll need to sand the planter with 120-grit sandpaper before you paint it. You'll find the grit printed on the back of the paper. Note that 120 grit is sometimes sold as medium paper with no grit size specified.

10| EXTERIOR-GRADE PRIMER & PAINT. You'll probably only need a quart of each.

11| EXTERIOR-GRADE WOOD FILLER. Fill in nail and screw holes before painting for a smooth, finished look.

12| VINYL LATTICE. Unlike wood lattice panels, these plastic panels won't rot and never need painting. Most home centers stock them in 4×8 size.

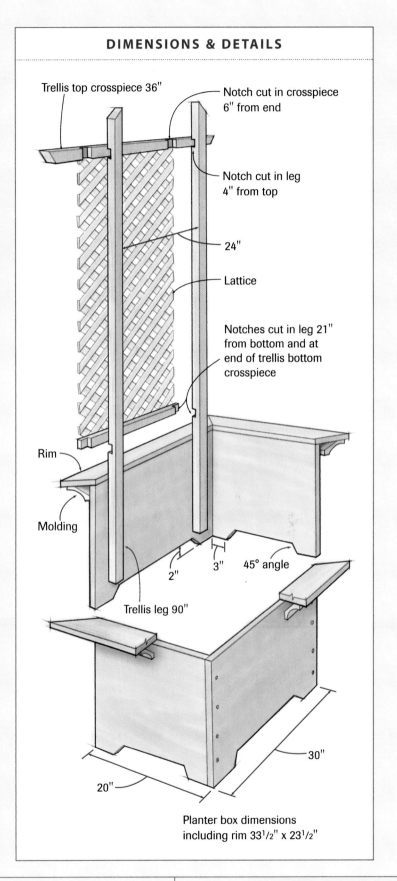

DIMENSIONS & DETAILS

Trellis top crosspiece 36"

Notch cut in crosspiece 6" from end

Notch cut in leg 4" from top

24"

Lattice

Notches cut in leg 21" from bottom and at end of trellis bottom crosspiece

Rim

Molding

Trellis leg 90"

2"

3"

45° angle

30"

20"

Planter box dimensions including rim 33½" x 23½"

Building the Planter

1 **CUT THE TOP & SIDES.** On the plywood, lay out the cuts for the planter box's top and sides. Remember to allow about ¼ in. between the pieces for the width of the sawblade. Cut out the pieces with your circular saw, using a saw guide to keep the cuts straight. Support the plywood with 2×4s or with sawhorses during cutting.

2 **LAY OUT THE FLOWERPOT HOLE.** Measure the flowerpot just below the rim to determine the hole size. (You want the rim to rest on the plywood so the pot hangs.) To find the center of the top, draw diagonal lines across it and mark where the lines cross. Measure out from  the center point along one of the diagonals half the measurement of the pot and mark. (This is where the outside of the circle will be.) Cut a string to the length between the marks. Nail the string to the center point and attach a pencil to the other end. To mark the round line for the circle, put the pencil on the mark and swing in a circle to lay out the hole.

3 **CUT OUT THE HOLE.** Drill a ⅜-in. hole just inside the circle. Insert the blade of your jigsaw through the hole. Cut along the line, following it as closely as possible. Don't worry if your cut wanders a little bit, because the rim of the pot will hide everything but the most serious disasters.

4 **CUT THE FEET.** Set your combination square at 2 in. Using the square as a guide, draw a line along the bottom edge of all four plywood sides. Once you've drawn the line,  lay out the feet at 45-degree angles as shown in the drawing on p. 93. Cut out a foot with the jigsaw, then cut toward the other foot along the pencil line and cut out the second foot. Repeat for all four pieces.

LINGO

Lap joints give this trellis frame a clean look. Notches are cut in intersecting pieces, which helps position the frame and hold it together. These joints are easy to assemble and strong.

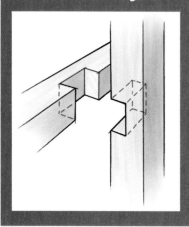

Building the Trellis

5 **CUT THE TRELLIS PIECES.** The trellis frame has two legs and top and bottom crosspieces. Cut the legs so they're 90 in. long. Cut the top crosspiece 36 in. long and the bottom crosspiece 24 in. long. The tops of the legs and the ends of the top crosspiece are cut at an angle. The exact measure of the angle isn't important. Set a T-bevel for what looks good, mark the pieces, and make the cuts.

6 **LAY OUT THE JOINTS.** All four of the frame pieces must have notches cut in them to make lap joints that hold the frame together (see LINGO at left). The legs are notched 4 in. from the top and 21 in. from the bottom. The top crosspiece is notched 6 in. from each end, and the bottom crosspiece is notched at the ends (see the drawing on p. 93). Lay out the notches with a combination square. The notch is as wide as a 2×2 (use a scrap of 2×2 to help you measure and mark). The notches should be half as deep as the board itself.

7 **CUT THE NOTCHES.** Adjust your circular saw's cutting depth so it will cut halfway through the 2×2s. Clamp the 2×2s together side by side in pairs—leg to leg and crosspiece to crosspiece. Clamp one of the pairs to your sawhorses. Make a series of closely spaced cuts to get rid of some of the material where the notches will be. Using a chisel, clean out the waste wood and smooth the bottom surface. Repeat on the remaining joints.

8 **ASSEMBLE THE FRAME.** Test-fit the joints and trim the pieces to fit if necessary. Spread polyurethane glue on the surfaces and put the frame together. Drill pilot holes through the pieces, then drive in 1¼-in. screws from the back of the frame. Nice work so far.

Assemble the Planter

9 **NOTCH THE PLANTER TOP.** The back edge of the planter's top needs to be notched so the trellis legs can slip inside. Center the top against the bottom of the trellis legs. Trace around the legs to lay out the notches, then cut the notches with your jigsaw. Follow the lines as best you can, but it's okay if the fit isn't perfectly tight.

10 **MAKE THE FIRST CORNER.** Start assembly by attaching the front of the planter to one of the sides. (Make sure you've got the best-looking side of the plywood facing out.) Draw a light line down the front, ⅜ in. in from the edge, to guide you as you drill for the screws. Clamp the pieces together and drill five pilot holes (⁵⁄₆₄ in. big) along the guideline. Drive 2-in. deck screws into the holes to fasten the pieces together.

11 **ATTACH THE TOP.** Draw a line 1½ in. below the top around the inside of the two pieces you just assembled. Set the top piece so its top is on the line and clamp it in place. Drill pilot holes, then screw the top in place through the front and side panels. Mark layout lines on the remaining side and on the back. Put them in place one at a time and screw them to the assembled sides and top.

12 **CUT THE RIM PIECES.** From the 1×3s, rough-cut the four rim pieces several inches longer than their finished dimensions. Miter one end of each. Have a helper hold each piece in place at the corner so you can mark where the opposite miter needs to be cut, and make the miter cuts. Clamp the rim to the box, drill pilot holes with a ¹⁄₁₆-in.-dia. bit, and then drive in 2-in. screws. Repeat all the way around the box.

⊙ DO IT RIGHT

Even though there are parts of the planter that won't show, paint everything anyway. Paint does more than simply make something look good. It also protects the wood from the weather. Your planter will last a lot longer if you take the time to paint the entire thing.

❋ DO IT FAST

Want to avoid painting and priming? Apply pigmented exterior stain, often called deck stain. It comes in a variety of colors. Brush it on and you're done. For a darker color and better protection, apply a second coat.

✛ SAFETY FIRST

If you use rags or a drop cloth while applying the paint or stain, hang them somewhere outside to dry. They're oil soaked and could ignite spontaneously, causing a serious fire.

Finishing Up

13 **ATTACH THE MOLDING.** As you did for the rims, miter one end of the molding, hold it in place under the rim, and mark the other end. Miter cut the end at the mark. Nail it in place with 3d finish nails.

14 **PRIME & PAINT.** Go over the entire planter and trellis frame with some 120-grit sandpaper to remove any splinters or rough spots. Apply a good-quality primer. Once the primer dries, apply your top coats. Use a putty knife to put wood filler in the nail and screw holes before you apply the final coat.

15 **CUT & ATTACH THE LATTICE.** After the paint dries, place the trellis frame on top of the lattice. Trace around the frame with a marker to show you where to cut the trellis. Cut the lattice to size with your circular saw. Screw the lattice to the back of the frame with round-head screws. For this project you'll drill pilot holes through the lattice that are bigger than the finish screws—³⁄₁₆ in. should be big enough—to give the lattice a little room to expand and contract.

16 **ATTACH THE TRELLIS.** Slip the trellis through the notches in the top of the planter, and clamp the legs in place if necessary. Measure at several points along the bottom crosspiece to make sure it is parallel to the top of the planter. Adjust if necessary. Drill ⁵⁄₆₄-in. pilot holes through the back of the planter. Then screw the trellis in place with three 2-in. screws per leg. You're done! Now you can pot your favorite climbing plant and get this project in grow mode.

Add instant vertical landscaping

with a trellis. Attached to a planter or to your house, a trellis provides firm support for climbing plants and adds a touch of architectural design to your landscape. Let the trellis make a statement in its design or color or play it down and let the climbing plants be the focal point.

A freestanding trellis attached to your house makes a great hangout for a climbing plant. Make the section of trellis that you sink into the ground at least half as long as the exposed section of trellis. Be sure to use rot-resistant wood or vinyl.

Make two trellis planters and turn them into an entryway by adding an arbor to the top.

A trellis can offer height to any planter. This one is sunken in the ground behind a half-whiskey barrel, allowing the climbers planted in the barrel to grow up.

Building your own planter box allows you to change its size to fit your space. The balusters on this deck railing act as a trellis.

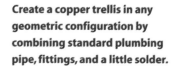
A simple trellis is easy to make if you don't like the premade options. Use 1x2 lumber rated for outdoor use and finish it or leave it natural. This painted trellis planter is a dramatic backdrop for the climbing plants.

Create a copper trellis in any geometric configuration by combining standard plumbing pipe, fittings, and a little solder.

103

Tabletop Water Fountain

Bring peace to any space with the sights & sounds
of this **WATER GARDEN**

YOU DON'T NEED A STREAM in your backyard—or a backyard for that matter—to enjoy the soothing sound of a babbling brook. Fortunately, there is a way to get the peaceful sound of trickling water without breaking the bank. With a small submersible pump, you can create your own container fountain that will gently burble in the background whether on your porch or in your living room. Even the best waterfront property won't do that.

TRIAL RUN	PREP THE FOCAL STONE	PUT IT BACK TOGETHER	FINISHING TOUCHES

Tools & Gear

Unless you choose to buy a predrilled focal stone, you'll need a drill and bits.

ELECTRIC DRILL. Some stone is so hard you may need a hammer drill (see COOL TOOL below), but in most cases a standard drill will do the job.

MASONRY DRILL BITS. Buy at least three different carbide-tipped masonry bits ranging from $\frac{1}{8}$-in. to $\frac{5}{6}$-in. diameters, or pick up a kit (index) that includes those sizes.

EYE PROTECTION. Stay safe. Always wear eye protection when drilling.

UTILITY KNIFE. Use this (or a single-edge razor blade) to cut plastic tubing to length.

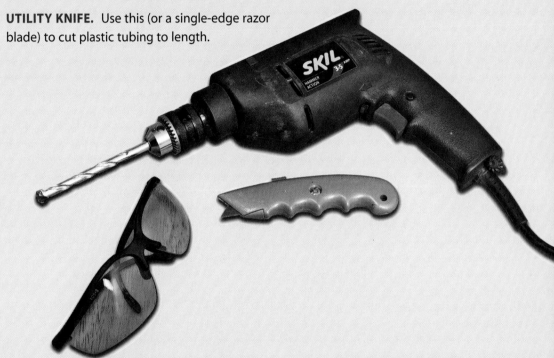

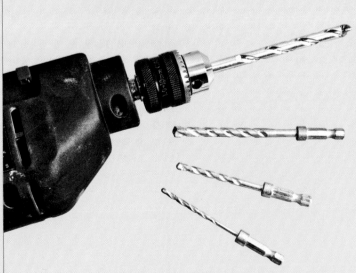

COOL TOOL

Drilling in very hard materials such as granite stone and certain tile can overheat, wear out, or break the tip of carbide masonry bits. A hammer drill can add a hammering action to the bit rotation that greatly speeds the work without damage or excessive bit wear.

What to Buy

1| CONTAINER. If your container is not waterproof, you will need to buy a second waterproof container that fits just inside the decorative one. (The glazed pot show in this project is waterproof.)

2| SUBMERSIBLE PUMP. You need a pump to deliver water to the top of your fountain. Suitable pumps are available in garden shops, craft stores and online. In addition to line voltage pumps there are low-voltage models and even battery-operated types.

3| STONES. You can buy bags of white or colored stones, or gather your own beauties from river beds and rock out-croppings. Wash the stones before you arrange them in your container.

4| CLEAR PLASTIC TUBING. This stuff is sold by the foot. Most small pumps accept ¼-in. tubing, and some suppliers include a length of tubing with your pump order.

SAFETY FIRST

To plug in a water fountain safely requires a special receptacle, called a ground fault circuit interrupter (GFCI). If you have an existing receptacle, you can tell it's a GFCI by the "Test" and "Reset" buttons. If you're using the fountain outdoors, you'll need an exterior GFCI outlet and a weather-proof box that protects the receptacle.

✳ DO IT NOW

After you attach the riser tube to the pump, place it in a sink or container of water, plug it in, and adjust the flow rate. Getting to the control knob after the rocks are in place can be tricky.

▶ DO IT RIGHT

Whenever drilling stone or other very hard materials with a masonry bit, start with an ⅛-in.-dia. bit and step up to the next size bit—no more than ⅛ in. at a time—until you achieve the desired diameter hole.

Making the Fountain

1 **TAKE A TRIAL RUN.** Arrange washed stones in the container to achieve a pleasing arrangement. Building up the stone at one corner is a good way to hide the water pump's power cord where it exits the container. Typically water is delivered through a hole in a stone near the top of the arrangement, so slope that stone toward the center.

2 **DRILL A HOLE IN FOCAL STONE.** Before you take apart your arrangement, mark the location on the focal stone for the hole you need to

drill for the plastic tubing. Using masonry bits and wearing eye protection, drill the hole in the focal stone. Place the rock on a lumber scrap and drill progressively larger holes, starting with ⅛-in. diameter, until you get to the size you need to fit the tubing. Remove the rest of the stones from the container so you can add the pump.

3 **RE-CREATE YOUR ARRANGEMENT.** Attach the tubing to the pump that will deliver the water up to the top of your fountain. Place the pump at the bottom of the container and surround it with a bed of small stones to hold it in place. Add the remaining stones. Feed the tubing through the hole you drilled in the focal stone and place it.

4 **RELAX AND ENJOY!** In this design, the final stone is placed over the water outlet to conceal the water source before the pump is plugged in.

This metal trough creates a focal point on the deck. Any metal container can work as a water garden. Just be sure to locate the pot in a shady spot, since metal heats up in the sun and can cook the roots of the plants.

Sometimes the most practical materials make the most unusual containers. Here copper plumbing pipe was used to form a hanger for a sheet of copper. Water runs up into the pipe, where holes were drilled to allow the water to trickle down the copper sheet and onto the stones below.

Contain your plants not your enthusiasm! Be creative when choosing a container for your water garden—anything that holds water will work. If you include plants, you can instantly redesign the planting arrangement by moving the submerged pots around. But don't feel like you have to include plants. Treat your ears—and mind—to the tranquility of the burps and gurgles of water as it moves through the container.

These water lilies are a perfect size for this small dish. While there are no strict design guidelines to follow when matching plants to containers, try to keep plants in scale with the container's size.

This water fountain features a plastic container buried underground that catches the falling water as it spills over the sides of the container. A pump recirculates the water back into the pot. The glaze of the pot is emphasized when wet.

Multi-Tier Container Stand

Build a three-step stage to showcase **YOUR POTTED PLANTS**

WITH A FEW WELL-CHOSEN containers and judicious use of a watering can, you can create a garden almost anywhere. But arranging the containers to show off their beauty is a different matter entirely. This nifty tiered stand allows you to create a multilevel array of foliage and flowers almost instantly. And since the steps use off-the-shelf materials available at any home center, you'll have them built in practically no time.

CUT THE STRINGER

LAY OUT SHELVES

ASSEMBLE

ATTACH SHELVES

The steps shown here are made from pressure-treated lumber. If you want rot-resistant wood that isn't chemically treated, try redwood or cedar. If your lumberyard doesn't have these naturally rot-resistant woods in stock, you can probably special-order some boards. If you go this route, chances are you'll have to make your own stringers by cutting out all the steps.

+ **SAFETY FIRST**

Treat pressure-treated wood with respect. The chemicals are benign in the wood and won't leach out, but sawing and burning release particles that you can ingest or inhale, which isn't good for you. Wear a dusk mask when cutting, wash the dust off your hands before eating, and take a shower when you're done working. Throw out wood scraps—don't burn them.

Tools & Gear

This project is pretty much straightforward carpentry and fairly basic carpentry at that. While there isn't much of an excuse here to buy any great new tools, you can always claim a need to upgrade.

TAPE MEASURE. You'll need a tape in order to lay out your cuts. Get one that is ¾ in. or even 1 in. wide. They're more durable than ½-in. tapes and less likely to bend while you're taking a measurement.

COMBINATION SQUARE. With a true right angle and a straight edge, a combination square is ideal for laying out perpendicular cuts.

CIRCULAR SAW. You're going to be making a few straight cuts. Although a handsaw will work, a circular saw makes the job go a lot faster. You'll find it handy for lots of other jobs, too.

DUST MASK. Whether you make your steps out of pressure-treated lumber or any other rot-resistant wood, the dust they'll produce is not something you want to suck into your lungs.

DRILL/DRIVER & BITS. Get a drill and a combination bit that drills a pilot hole and a recess for the screw head in one pass. While you're at it, get a screwdriver bit for the drill to make quick work of driving the screws.

What to Buy

1| STAIR STRINGERS. You can usually find precut stair stringers in the same aisle as fence posts or deck parts. They come in four- and six-step lengths. Get two of the six-step stringers: You'll cut them into two three-step pieces.

2| 2×6. The piece that ties two of the stringers together is made from a short piece of 2×6. See if you can find a scrap about 15 in. long. If not, buy as short a piece as you can talk the lumber guy out of. (He's probably got a bin of short pieces somewhere.)

3| 1×2s. You'll need two 8-ft. pieces for the shelves.

4| SCREWS. You'll need about half a pound of 2½-in. deck screws, either galvanized or ceramic coated.

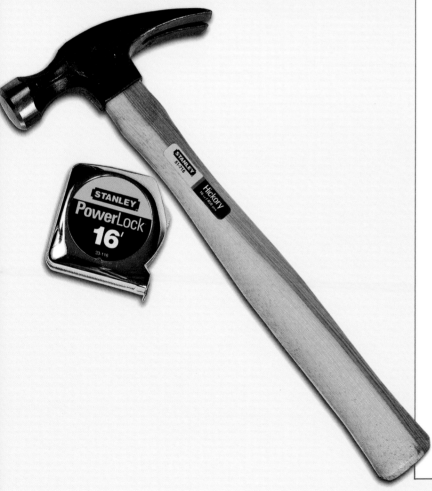

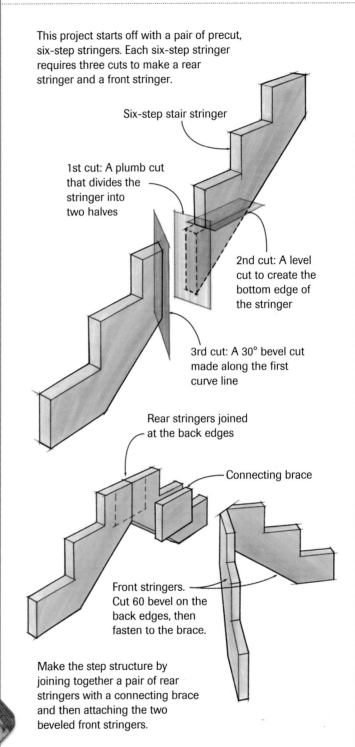

CUTTING & ASSEMBLING THE STAIR STRINGERS

This project starts off with a pair of precut, six-step stringers. Each six-step stringer requires three cuts to make a rear stringer and a front stringer.

Six-step stair stringer

1st cut: A plumb cut that divides the stringer into two halves

2nd cut: A level cut to create the bottom edge of the stringer

3rd cut: A 30° bevel cut made along the first curve line

Rear stringers joined at the back edges

Connecting brace

Front stringers. Cut 60 bevel on the back edges, then fasten to the brace.

Make the step structure by joining together a pair of rear stringers with a connecting brace and then attaching the two beveled front stringers.

■ **LINGO**

The "run" on a stairway is the distance from the front to the back of a step, minus any overhang. The distance each step goes up is called the rise.

✛ **WHAT CAN GO WRONG**

In the heat of construction, it is quite easy to forget and make two duplicate parts instead of a right and a left side. The correct cuts are shown above. If you goof and make two identical parts, don't fret. Find the cutoff piece and glue it back in place. Drive in a couple of screws to serve as clamps. When the glue dries, back out the screws and recut the bevel going in the proper direction.

Cutting the Stringers

1 **LAY OUT THE FIRST CUT.** As shown in the drawing on p. 115, each six-step stringer requires three cuts to create one three-step rear stringer and one three-step front stringer. Lay out the first cut by measuring the run (step width) of the uppermost step. Then subtract 1½ in. (the thickness of your brace) and transfer this length to the run of the fourth step.

2 **MAKE THE FIRST CUT.** Use a square to mark a plumb cut line from the mark you made in step 1. This is a "plumb" cut because it will eventually end up in a vertical position. Cut along this line with a circular saw. Make sure to wear eye protection and a dust mask.

3 **MAKE THE SECOND CUT.** This is a level cut that will complete one of the rear stringers. A good way to mark or lay out this cut is to stack the bottom half of the stringer on the top half so that the steps align, then mark along the bottom. Use your circular saw to make the cut.

4 **MAKE THE THIRD CUT.** This cut creates a 60-degree bevel along the plumb cut you made in step 2. Tilt the blade on your circular saw to 60 degrees, and cut the bevel. Good job so far. Now repeat these steps on the other six-step stringer. Remember that the front stringer you cut this time needs to have its bevel going in the opposite direction.

While it is possible to drive deck screws into materials without pilot holes, it is not a very good idea. Without a pilot hole you run the risk of either splitting the wood or snapping the screw off. While it takes a little extra time, drilling a pilot hole (usually $3/32$ in. – $1/8$ in. dia.) eliminates these risks and allows the pieces to draw nicely together. Use a combination bit to drill a pilot hole and a recess for the screw head, called a countersink.

When drilling the pilot holes for attaching the beveled stringers to the connecting piece, the holes should be perpendicular to the beveled surface. Rather than trying to drill a hole at an angle, turn the piece around and drill from the beveled side where you can hold the drill perpendicular to the surface.

Assembling the Shelves

5 **CONNECT THE TWO REAR STRINGERS.** Cut a connecting brace from some 2×6 lumber. You can make this brace about 16 in. long. Take the two rear stringers and place them back to back as shown in the drawing on p. 115. Glue your connecting brace over the joint, using construction adhesive. Center the brace, and screw it in place with four 2½-in. deck screws per side. You'll find it easier to drive the screws if you drill pilot holes first.

6 **ATTACH THE BEVELED STRINGERS.** Use a square and a pencil to draw a line across the center of the connecting brace so that you can align each beveled stringer. Hold the first stringer in place, with its beveled plumb cut on your layout line, and predrill pilot holes for three 2½-in. deck screws. Drive the screws to fasten the beveled stringer to the brace. Install the remaining stringer the same way.

7 **LAY OUT THE SHELVES.** Your stringer structure is complete; it's time to cut and install the shelves. Cut a 2×10 into three 32-in.-long pieces that you'll use for the bottom shelf pieces. Cut the other 2×10 into four 22-in.-long pieces. With a pencil and square,

mark a centerline on the front edges of the two front stringers. Then, starting on a bottom shelf, place one of the 32-in. shelf pieces on the stringers. Mark each edge where it crosses the centerlines you drew. Connect these marks with a straightedge to establish cut lines for the bottom shelf pieces. Then do the same thing for the second-level shelf pieces, working with your 22-in.-long pieces.

8 **CUT & ATTACH THE SHELVES.** Cut along the layout lines and put the shelves in place so you don't lose track of the layout. Then mark and cut the top shelf from your remaining 22-in. piece of 2×10. Install each shelf piece with 2½-in. deck screws. Make sure to drill pilot holes for your screws so you don't split the wood.

The mass of tiered plantings takes full advantage of this intimate patio space. The positioning of the containers allows the drama to be viewed from inside the house, too.

Step beyond the basic design.

Precut materials make it easy to tailor-make shelves. Alter the design to suit your space and style—make your stairs taller or wider, with fewer sides or curved stringers. The same basic construction techniques and principles apply.

Empty containers turned upside down simulate the step effect. Vary the height and materials of the base containers for drama. Be sure the upsidedown container is heavy enough to support the filled container.

Paint or stain the steps so that the structure stands out against the colors of the plants and landscape.

Curved "stringers" and white paint add elegance to this set of stairs.

For more great weekend project ideas look for these and other
TAUNTON PRESS BOOKS wherever books are sold.

Patios and Walkways
ISBN 1-56158-723-0
Product #070813
$14.95

Paint Transformations
ISBN 1-56158-670-6
Product #070751
$14.95

Lighting Solutions
ISBN 1-56158-669-2
Product #070753
$14.95

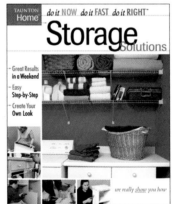

Trim Transformations
ISBN 1-56158-671-4
Product #070752
$14.95

Storage Solutions
ISBN 1-56158-668-4
Product #070754
$14.95

For more information visit our Web site at www.doitnowfastright.com